dancing in the aisle

dancing in the aisle

Spiritual Lessons

We've Learned

from Children

Rochelle Melander and Harold Eppley

United Church Press
Cleveland, Ohio

United Church Press, Cleveland, Ohio 44115

© 1999 by Rochelle Melander and Harold Eppley

These stories and incidents are true. Names, locations, and identifying details have been changed to protect the identities of persons who appear in this book.

Unless otherwise specified, biblical quotations are from the New Revised Standard Version of the Bible, © 1989 by the Division of Christian Education of the National Council of Churches of Christ in the U.S.A., and are used by permission. Adaptations have been made for inclusivity.

Printed in the United States of America on acid-free paper

04   03   02   01   00   99   5   4   3   2   1

Library of Congress Cataloging-in-Publication Data

Melander, Rochelle.

  Dancing in the aisle : spiritual lessons we've learned from children / Rochelle Melander and Harold Eppley.

    p.   cm.

  ISBN 0-8298-1352-7 (pbk. : alk. paper)

  1. Christian life—United Church of Christ authors.   2. Children—Religious life.   I. Eppley, Harold.   I. Title.

  BV4509.5.M45   1999

  259' .22—dc21   99-30817

                                                              CIP

For Samuel—

even when you're as old as your parents,

you'll still be a child in the eyes of God.

Contents

Acknowledgments

Both of us heard God's call to write early in life. The process of responding to God's call and actually creating a book requires the support and care of many people.

We thank our families, friends, and colleagues who recognized our literary gifts and nurtured them. We appreciate all of you who have encouraged, challenged, and inspired us through the years—especially Siiri Branstrom-Peters, Debra Brenegan, the Carlson family, Karen Church, Rebekah Eppley, Jan Ewing, Cynthia Fazzini, Nick Fisher-Broin, Kip Groettum, Brad Kmoch, Ellen Meissgeier, Chris Melander, MaryJo Melander, Lester Meyer, Donnita Moeller, Bonnie Peterson, Dawn Pomento, Steve Rye, Andrea Lee Schieber, Serena Sellers, Peggy Tromblay, Helen Wasuck, and our parents, Dick and Diane Melander and Samuel and Linda Eppley.

We would like to thank all those on the staff of United Church Press who have expressed enthusiasm for this project and offered their unique gifts to shape our stories into a beautiful book. We'd especially like to thank Kim Sadler, Ed Huddleston, Martha Clark, and Madrid Tramble.

As children we spent many holiday meals sitting at the "children's table," protected from adult conversation (and safely away from the valuable family china). In those days we yearned to be able to sit with the "grown-ups," privy to their secret stories. Now that we are adults, we long to be back at the children's table. Thankfully, we have been blessed with the friendship of many children. And because of that, we sometimes still have the privilege of "sitting with the kids," listening to their stories, and joining in their play. We have written this book because of you children, too numerous to name, who have ministered to us by being who God has called you to be. You have blessed us beyond measure. We hope that through this book, the witness of your words and lives will be a blessing to many others.

How to Use This Book

You may use the meditations in this book for your own personal reflection or for a tool for discussion with your family or church group. Each meditation begins with a suggested scripture reading that you may use to center yourself or the group. The meditation concludes with questions that encourage you to reflect on your spiritual life. The questions can be used as a way to spur individual reflection (either thinking silently or writing thoughts in a journal) or as a guide to group discussion. The challenge exercise provides an opportunity for you to further consider how the insights raised in the meditation can be applied to your spiritual journey.

Introduction

On a cold Ash Wednesday evening, just days before our first child was born, we worshiped with a friend and her family. Our friend's five-year-old daughter was learning to read, and she liked it when her mother pointed to each word in the worship book. It helped her to follow the service. That night she wanted to share a book with us. She asked us to point to the text, marking each word as we read or sang it. We obediently opened the hymnal to the appropriate page and pointed. Together we spoke and sang the words of worship. And we learned about paying attention.

As pastors, we're usually leading the worship service. Most often we're simply reciting the words we have memorized. We neglect to attend to what we are saying to God because we are noticing that the acolyte forgot to light one of the candles. We are distracted by the wayward child who has made her way into the pulpit again. Friends who are not pastors say that they, too, have trouble paying attention in church. Sometimes the distracting sighs and cries of children draw their focus away from God; other times the constant demands of their lives creep in to interrupt their meditation.

That evening, after the service, we talked together about the experience of helping our five-year-old friend to read from the hymnal. We realized that she had unwittingly served as our spiritual guide by helping us to focus our attention on the words we were speaking to God. We were fascinated by the fact that a five-year-old could teach two pastors something about their own spirituality. And we thought about all the times we fail to pay attention—not only to God, but also to

, including the children in our midst. In that con-
.., the idea for this book was born. We wondered what
other spiritual lessons we had learned from children and how
our own child would instruct us.

In the following months, we started to pay closer attention to
the many children we encountered in our churches and in our
community. As we began to collect stories, we realized that listening to the voices of children is a lot like listening to the
voice of God—there are some things that are pleasant to hear
and other messages that we'd prefer to ignore. If you're a
parent or have ever spent time with children, you know what
we mean. Sometimes we hear the children's voices, and it's like
hot fudge being poured over ice cream. We devour the giggles
and sweet sayings of our little friends. Other times it's more
like the sound of fingernails on a chalkboard. We cringe at the
bedtime temper tantrums, the exhausted and irrational midday
whines, the cruel words shouted in moments of anger. Being in
relationship with children delivers a mixed bag of blessings and
challenges.

Yet if we listen closely to children's voices, if we pay attention to their actions and habits, if we reflect on the stories they
tell us about their lives, we learn something about our own
journey of faith. In the Scriptures God told the young prophet
Jeremiah: "Do not say, 'I am only a child.' . . . I have put my
words in your mouth . . . to uproot and tear down, to destroy
and overthrow, to build and to plant" (Jer. 1:7, 9–10 NIV).

Though our relationship with God takes many forms, it is
always in its very essence most akin to that of a child with a
parent. Throughout the Scriptures, people of all ages are
referred to as "children" or "children of God." The writer of
Psalm 103 declared, "As a father has compassion for his children, so God has compassion for those who fear God" (v. 13).

The prophet Hosea portrayed God as a tender and loving parent who taught the child Israel to walk and grieved when Israel turned away (Hos. 11). Jesus used the image of a mother hen gathering her brood under her wings to describe his own relationship with the residents of Jerusalem (Luke 13:34).

This book reflects upon what the experiences of children have taught us and others about our relationship with God and the community of faith. We have discovered that children and adults face many of the same basic spiritual issues. We encounter and affirm the challenges and insights of childhood throughout all the ages and stages of our lives.

We hope that the observations in this book will help you learn something about your journey with God. We trust you will be challenged to pay closer attention to the children who touch your life and reflect on the lessons their experiences can teach you.

1

Dancing in the Aisle

Mark 14:3–9

A few years ago we attended a service at a small church in the country. When the congregation began to sing, a little girl with bouncing curly brown hair and a twirling red skirt rose from her seat, headed for the center aisle, and began to dance. With arms lifted high, the tiny creature spun and kicked and swayed to the hymn. And as she danced, her face beamed. It wasn't just the smile. It was how her eyes sparkled and her skin glowed. The child's heart seemed to be filled with pure joy.

Almost as soon as the girl began to dance, her mother whispered repeatedly, "Eva, come back and sit down!" The girl with the bouncing hair kept dancing. Finally, the mother stomped into the aisle, grabbed the girl's hand, and led her out of church.

On another occasion we were walking in the mall, pushing our nine-month-old son, Samuel, in his stroller. Samuel was giggling, enjoying the ride, enthralled by all the people passing by. When we stopped to look in a store window, he began to fuss, annoyed by the sudden lack of movement.

A young girl, her brown face surrounded by braids held together with a rainbow of barrettes, walked up to Samuel and kissed his pale bald head. She patted his tiny hand and said, "Don't cry, little baby." Samuel cooed at her. He forgot his tears as he flirted with his new friend.

Then the girl's father appeared. "Shaina, don't go kissing other people's babies," he said as he pulled Samuel's new friend away. The father headed toward the other end of the mall, dragging the little girl behind him. As they left, Shaina turned and, in a final affectionate gesture, raised her hand to her lips and blew a kiss to Samuel.

The Gospel writer Mark told about a woman who, like Eva and Shaina, was chastised for her extravagant behavior. According to Mark, this woman entered the house of Simon the leper and dumped costly perfume on Jesus' head as a sign of affection for him, a sort of goodbye gift before his impending death. The dinner guests scolded her. They made the very practical suggestion that the perfume could have been sold and the money given to the poor. Instead of agreeing with their politically correct notion, Jesus commended the woman's action. He said, "Wherever the good news is proclaimed in the whole world, what she has done will be told in remembrance of her" (Mark 14:9).

The text left out much of the details. The woman was not named. The text did not reveal how the unnamed woman decided to anoint Jesus. One fact is clear: those dining with Jesus deemed the woman's act to be extravagant in the truest sense of the word. ("Extravagant" comes from a word that literally means "to wander beyond bounds.")

We live in a world concerned with boundaries and rules. At some point in our lives most of us have learned that doing anything outside the norm is seen as strange or wrong. No doubt, boundaries and rules serve an important function in our society. They help to keep order. Part of the process of "growing up" is learning appropriate social behavior. However, as adults, we sometimes become so conscious of society's restraints that our impulses to act lovingly can be squelched before they are even born. Like Eva's mother and Shaina's father, we may become embarrassed and ashamed when we witness uncensored love and affection. Sometimes we fear the reproach of others. Perhaps Eva's mother worried that the other worshipers might complain. And maybe Shaina's father feared that we would be upset by a stranger kissing our baby, passing her toddler germs to our new child.

A scribe once asked Jesus which commandment was "the first of all" (Mark 12:28). Jesus' response held this basic message: love God with all your being and love your neighbor as yourself. In other words, love extravagantly. In his own life Jesus demonstrated what he meant. When he healed on the Sabbath, when he touched people considered to be unclean, when he forgave sinners and dined with them, Jesus loved in ways that broke down boundaries and challenged the normative standards of his day.

Clearly, both Eva and Shaina hadn't lived long enough for society's rules of proper public conduct to be embedded in their minds. They were still young enough to act with loving impulses. In their moments of passion, as they listened to their hearts, they fulfilled Jesus' command to love God and others in ways that challenge social boundaries.

Sometimes it takes folks from the very edge of society—children and an unnamed woman—to challenge our obsession with the rules of proper conduct, to breathe grace and joy and freedom into our lives. Sometimes we need to witness the kiss of a little girl wiping away the sadness of a crying baby in order to envision a world without so many boundaries. Some days we need to see a child dancing in the aisle to encourage us to follow our hearts.

Questions for Reflection or Discussion

1. Recall a time when your heart urged you to do something spontaneous, but you resisted. What held you back?
2. Recall a time when you didn't hold back. What allowed you to follow your heart? What happened?
3. Have you become more or less concerned about the opinions of others as you've grown in years? What factors have influenced your attitudes?

Challenge

Think about activities you've always wanted to try but haven't because you have feared that others would disapprove.

Write down three of these activities.

Choose one of them to do this week.

Afterward, reflect on the experience in a journal or with a friend using the following questions as a guide:

What kinds of emotions did you have before the experience? During the experience? After the experience?

Has the experience affected the way you live? How?

Are there other activities you would like to try in the future? Which ones?

2

Why?

P s a l m   8 8 : 9 – 1 4

Why, Mommy? Why do birds fly?"

"Why, Daddy? Why can't my dog talk?"

"Grandma, why do we have hair on the top of our heads but not on the bottom of our feet?"

Most children pass through a stage that could be described as the "age of many questions." It's that time somewhere between the ages of three and six when children are first discovering the world in which they live and seeking to make some sense of it. Trying to satisfy these children's curiosity is like attempting to hold back floodwaters with an umbrella.

We pity the adults who aspire to respond to this deluge of questions. By the time they have finished explaining the differences between animals and humans, the child has moved on to even more perplexing problems. Why do people hurt each other? Why did Grandpa die? Why do some mommies and daddies divorce? What does God look like? Some adults try to answer these questions with logical explanations. Others shrug their shoulders and admit to being stumped. Most children are not satisfied with simple answers, statements such as, "That's just the way it is," or "Only God knows." And so the questions keep coming.

A friend of ours confessed that she found herself replying to her son's many questions with the same unsatisfactory answers her parents had given her twenty-five years before. One day her son defiantly demanded, "Why do I have to pick up my toys?" Our friend placed her hands on her hips and, in the tone she had often heard her mother use, bellowed, *"Because I said so . . . that's why!"*

Of course, children aren't the only ones who ask difficult questions. We all do. We live in a world filled with violence and senseless accidents. Anyone watching the nightly news might ask, "Where is a loving God in the midst of all this pain and suffering?" Any person who has experienced injustice or rejection might wonder how God can permit so much unfairness in the world.

We aren't the first to question God. When God called to Moses to speak to the pharaoh and lead the people out of Israel, Moses had many questions: "Who am I? . . . Suppose they do not believe me or listen to me?" (Exod. 3:11; 4:1). The writers of the Psalms also posed questions: "O God, why do you cast me off? Why do you hide your face from me?" (Ps. 88:14). Even Jesus questioned God. Just before his death, Jesus cried out, "My God, my God, why have you forsaken me?" (Matt. 27:46).

God has created a universe in which the answers to life's perplexing questions are not always immediately apparent. Even so, many of us yearn for a God who would outfit each of us at birth with a guidebook to life. The guide would provide us with proof for the existence of God, answers to any questions that might surface, explanations for our trials and tribulations, and even some suggested solutions. But we don't live in a world like that. God doesn't give us an answer key for the questions of life. For it is in not knowing the answers that we find the motive to study and learn. It's when we face our doubts and ask the tough questions that we grow in our faith.

We have noticed that like children, adults who take their Christian life seriously often ask a lot of questions. Most of us don't spend much time questioning the trivial matters in our lives, for example, choosing which pair of socks to wear or which brand of cereal to eat for breakfast. We spend the most time wondering about and questioning and even doubting the important decisions. Are we choosing the right home, the right career, the right person to marry? The meaningful matters need the most examination. And we don't decide what to do without first asking and pondering the difficult questions.

Jesus calls us to be his disciples, to take up our cross and follow him. If we take that task seriously, if we earnestly desire to live the Christian life, then we will occasionally have questions and doubts about what Jesus is calling us to be and do in this world. And as we grow in faith, we will start to see that following Jesus doesn't give us all the right answers. It teaches us to ask the right questions.

At the end of his career the famous theologian Karl Barth, who wrote voluminously about God and the Christian faith, was reportedly asked, "In all that you have studied, what is the most important thing you have learned?" Barth responded by reciting a favorite children's song: "Jesus loves me, this I know, for the Bible tells me so." It is the same for us. Even though many of our questions remain unanswered, and we cannot completely understand God's ways, we do know that God loves us. Why? Because the Bible tells us so. (Because God said so . . . that's why!) It may not be the answer we want. But for now, it is the best answer we have.

Questions for Reflection or Discussion

1. Recall a time when you had to make an important decision. How did asking questions help? What else was useful to you?
2. What is one belief or practice in the Christian faith that you depend on to help you in the midst of asking difficult questions?
3. If you could ask God three questions, what would they be?

Challenge

Look at the questions you noted to respond to number three above. Choose one of them and try to find an answer. You may choose to consult books, a theological teacher, or other spiritual leader. Beware! You may not discover a concrete, final answer. (But do enjoy the journey of seeking.)

3

Teenage Tumbleweed

Jeremiah 17:5–8

Thirteen-year-old Lisa transformed her appearance with the frequency that most of us wash our clothes. She did it to fit in—with her new boyfriend, with her girlfriends, with whichever group she happened to be associating at the moment. The first time we met Lisa, she was dating the captain of the debate team. She dressed conservatively, every strand of her long blonde hair in place. Just a few weeks later, Lisa came to church with her hair cut short, spiked straight up, and dyed blue, purple, and green. Her tattered tee shirt and well-worn jeans matched the colors in her hair. However, this transformation didn't last long, either. Soon it was replaced by yet another look, geared to garner acceptance and love from someone new.

Lisa's physical appearance wasn't the only part of her life that changed. Each time her community changed, so did her interests and preferences. Lisa so longed for the acceptance of others that she literally changed her person to find welcome. Lisa didn't possess the confidence to trust that being herself was enough.

Our hearts bled for Lisa. We liked the real Lisa immensely, the Lisa of whom we caught a glimpse only irregularly. But Lisa was neither content nor comfortable with herself. She felt certain that she could not measure up to others' expectations. Perhaps we felt so sad about Lisa because we, too, have faced Lisa's dilemma. We have wanted to feel accepted and loved, and yet we don't always trust that who we are, by God's design and nurturing, is quite good enough.

Television, movies, and magazines have bombarded us all with images of beauty and success. We see glamorous people living their glorious lives, and we may feel that we don't entirely measure up to the standards set before us. Our society's obsession with the rich and famous suggests that we all should be farther along in our journey to worldly success. We're constantly tempted to strive for what we don't possess, whether it is material goods, physical beauty, or love. Being content with who we are at this moment is difficult.

This dis-ease with ourselves, with our person, cannot be fixed by changing ourselves. Chances are, if we don't learn to love ourselves as we are today, no amount of change will satisfy us. We can make over our hair and clothes, we can redecorate our lives, we can take on new careers, we can fix it all—and it won't bring us contentment. We need to look deeper, beneath the surface of our lives, to discover the cause of our dis-ease.

The prophet Jeremiah spoke about this difficulty. He said that those who do not trust in God are like plants without roots. In prairie lands where the climate is dry, the ground is covered by a plant that the local people call Russian thistle. When moisture levels are low, branches from the Russian thistle break off from its roots and become tumbleweeds. As the cold wind blows across the prairie, these tumbleweeds are tossed through the air. They sail for miles in whichever direction the wind is blowing. Tumbleweeds are rootless—like those of us who are not anchored in God.

Jeremiah went on to compare those who trust in God with trees planted by water, rooted and nourished by the stream. The trees flourished regardless of external circumstances. Being content with who we are means being rooted in God— fed by God's Word and nurtured by the community of faith.

People who are rooted don't have perfect lives and are not beautiful and happy all the time. It's just that in whatever situation they face, they possess a secure sense that they belong to God and that they are accepted by God just the way they are. This acceptance enables them to face life's most difficult challenges with both courage and confidence.

Jesus doesn't ask Christians to change to please him. Jesus loves us as we are. Jesus sees us, blemishes and all, and calls us beautiful. Jesus knows our deepest insecurities, our secrets and fears, and yet never fails to embrace us. Jesus' love gives us the roots to stand firm in an ever-changing world. Jesus' love reminds us that we belong to God and, like trees planted by water, we will flourish through all the seasons of our lives.

Questions for Reflection or Discussion

1. What messages do you receive about how you "should" look, act, think, and feel from the following sources: the media, the church, your family, your friends, and your coworkers?

2. Think of a person whom you admire for being "rooted" in his or her faith. What are the person's qualities that enable him or her to be "rooted"?

3. Name a person who has accepted you unconditionally. How has that acceptance helped you in life?

Challenge

Are you rooted in the faith or tossing in the wind?

Divide a sheet of paper into three columns. Write these headings at the top of the columns: "Rooted," "Tossing," "Resources." In the first and second columns, list evidence for each in your life. For example, in the "Rooted" column, you might write "attend church regularly." In the "Tossing" column, you might list "tend to speak differently about myself depending upon whom I'm with." This will give you a good idea about how rooted you are.

When you have completed the first two columns, fill in the third column with a list of your resources for being rooted in the faith. Before you put this piece of paper away, reflect on how you can make better use of these resources for rootedness.

Thank-You Note

1 Thessalonians 5:16–18

Eleven-year-old Chad faced a predicament—how to say thank you when he didn't feel thankful. It was no simple problem. Chad had received an unwanted Christmas gift from his grandmother, a woman with whom he shared a close and enduring relationship.

Chad and his siblings had come to expect that on their birthdays and holidays, they would receive a unique homemade gift from their grandmother. Grandma had a knack for designing personalized clothing for each of her grandchildren, which most often they wore with pride. This year, however, her creation for Chad had fallen short of the usual standards.

After much consideration, Chad solved his predicament by carefully constructing his thank-you note. He wrote:

Dear Grandma, I received the red shirt you sent me for Christmas. How are you? I am fine. By the way, did you know that my favorite color is blue? Also, most people my age (almost a teenager) don't wear shirts with their initials sewn on them. I hope you don't think I am being ungrateful or anything (because I'm not).

Grandma, you and I have known each other for a long time now, and you've always told me to be honest with you. So I just thought I'd give you a few pointers. Please don't be mad at me. You are the best grandma in the whole world (I mean it!!!). THANK YOU FOR BEING MY GRANDMA!!!

Love, Chad

P.S. Some of my friends' grandparents give them money for Christmas.

How do we say thank you when we don't feel thankful? It's a problem with which most of us occasionally struggle. Especially in our relationship with God, we may feel hard-pressed to speak words of gratitude when we're not totally pleased with the gifts God has given us. When the supper we over-cooked tastes like the aftermath of a nuclear meltdown, when the telephone keeps ringing and our children won't stop screaming, when it has rained for three days and the basement is flooding, a prayer of thanks for our daily blessings may sound a bit insincere.

Like Chad, we don't always get what we want. We may wish that God had made a less prominent nose or thicker hair. If we could ask God for exactly what we wanted, we might request a more patient temperament, a more agile body, or quicker wits. Most of us would like to change at least a few of the details in our lives.

How do we say thank you when we don't feel thankful? The apostle Paul encouraged Christians to "rejoice always" and "give thanks in all circumstances" (1 Thess. 5:16, 18). Paul was able to write these words even though he encountered great suffering and misfortune. Over the course of his lifetime Paul was imprisoned, shipwrecked, persecuted, and plagued by a mysterious ailment that he referred to as "a thorn in the flesh." Several times Paul asked God to remove these problems from his life. God did not.

Like Chad, Paul was able to express gratitude because he realized that ultimately, our relationships are the most valuable treasures of our lives. Though Chad couldn't find room in his heart to thank his grandmother for the red shirt, he still was able to unabashedly exclaim, THANK YOU FOR BEING MY GRANDMA! Though Paul's troubles continued to plague him throughout his life, he proclaimed, "Thanks be to God, who in Christ . . . spreads in every place the fragrance that comes from knowing God" (2 Cor. 2:14).

We may not feel up to thanking God for our homes when the ceilings are leaking or for the beauty of a spring day when we're allergic to flowering plants. Yet we can always thank God for daily loving us, relating to us, and supporting us through all the circumstances of our lives. Even on the worst of days, we can say with confidence, THANK YOU FOR BEING MY GOD!

Questions for Reflection or Discussion

1. Recall someone who has remained thankful in the midst of a difficult situation. In what ways is his or her example helpful to you?
2. When do you find it difficult to be thankful?
3. What enables you (or those you know) to maintain a grateful attitude?

Challenge

Write a thank-you note to God. Be honest.

5

Sticks and Stones

1 Peter 4:8−11

Lin came home from school one day with a frown on her face. Later, Lin's mother found that she had dumped all of her art supplies and drawings in the trash.

When asked why, Lin replied, "For art I drew our purple tree."

"You mean the lilacs?" asked Lin's mother.

"Yes, and my teacher said that there was no such thing as a tree with purple leaves. And then she told me, 'Why not make a green tree like Marjorie has done?' I am never going to draw again," wailed Lin.

At the mall, we overheard a normal-sized teenage girl moaning to her mother, "Mom, the coach said I was fat, and she was right. Look at me! Everything I wear looks disgusting."

On the playground, we heard a group of young children exchanging insults with one another. Mostly, they were calling one another names. "Rat," "meatball," "rabbit-brain"—the insults flew at a rapid pace. Before long, we heard the familiar rhyme we learned as children, shouted in the shrill voice of a child trying to conceal his emotions. "Sticks and stones may break my bones, but words will never hurt me."

Words can hurt, and words can heal. Sometimes it seems that the hurting words stay with us longer than the healing words. The hurting words seep like sewage into our minds, polluting our thinking: *There are no such things as purple trees. You're fat. Rat, meatball, rabbit-brain!* Soon we add our own thoughts to these: *She's right; I can't draw at all. I am really ugly. How could I be so stupid?* Before long, these word-spears have wounded our hearts, and we bleed.

Words can hurt, and they can heal. Sometimes all it takes is a kind word from another person to lift us out of our doldrums. A number of successful people have attributed their persistence in the face of rejection to the encouraging comments of one or two others. And many people have experienced how mending words, uttered at the right time, can heal a relationship. Our spouses, or our friends, having wronged us, simply say, "I'm sorry," and the pain is immediately deadened. We embrace and begin the hard work of healing. But the few kind words—they are the beginning, the first sensation of ointment on an open wound.

The writer of Ephesians declared, "Let no evil talk come out of your mouths, but only what is useful for building up, as there is need, so that your words may give grace to those who hear" (Eph. 4:29). This wonderful passage could be printed in a modern advice column. "Tell me what to do, dear Abby. I am having problems in my marriage. We just don't communicate anymore." The answer? "Watch the way you talk. Let nothing foul or dirty come out of your mouth. Say only what helps, each word a gift" (Eph. 4:29, from *The New Testament in Contemporary Language* by Eugene Peterson).

How different our lives would be if somehow we could program that verse into our brain processors. Then, before we spoke, before we said what was burning in our mouths, we would stop and think: *Will what I am saying build up, will it deliver grace to those who hear, or will it be like evil, shooting out of my mouth to destroy another soul?* Maybe the key is to be aware—to be cognizant of the fact that words have an effect. They can tear down, and they can also build up. They can bring evil, and they can also be vehicles of grace.

Often Jesus' words conveyed grace to the hearers. People who expected condemnation, who had lived for many years with the curses of others, received far different treatment from Jesus. In Mark's Gospel, a woman plagued by a twelve-year flow of blood touched the hem of Jesus' garment and was made well (Mark 5:25–34). Jesus, knowing that power had left him, asked, "Who touched my clothes?" (Mark 5:30). In fear and trembling (for she must have known that her bleeding made her unclean and untouchable), the woman knelt down before Jesus and "told him the whole truth" (Mark 5:33). Jesus could have cursed her. The touch of a bleeding woman would have made a Jewish male unclean. Jewish men were instructed to say to such a woman, "Be gone, filthy woman." Instead, Jesus said, "Daughter, your faith has made you well; go in peace, and be healed of your disease" (Mark 5:34). He spoke to her as a loving parent to a child. He gave her the benediction for which she had hoped—healing.

The chant about sticks and stones that many of us recited as children was simply and wholly wrong. Words don't float out of our mouths into an abyss. Wicked words shoot like pointed and poisonous arrows, straight into the soul of the hearer. In contrast, our kind words shower love like a warm spring rain onto the hearer, bringing growth and greater beauty. When we realize this, we think before we speak. We speak with each hearer's heart and goodwill in mind. And we seek out others who will nourish us with kind words of their own.

Questions for Reflection or Discussion

1. When have you been hurt by someone else's words? How did this experience affect your relationship with the person?

2. When have you been encouraged by another's kind words? How did this affect you?

3. Recall a time when your words had an unexpected effect on someone else (either positive or negative). What did you learn from that experience?

Challenge

Each day many of us overlook opportunities to praise others. We also receive compliments that we brush off or don't hear.

Resolve to give and receive three compliments each day this week.

Keep a journal of these compliments as a record for yourself.

At the end of the week, look at the journal, and examine how you felt when you gave and received compliments.

Did this experience change your perspective about yourself or others?

6

Holy Play

Psalm 148

We officiated at a wedding the other day. The bride wore a long lace veil and a stunning ivory dress with a train. The bride's older sister was the beaming attendant, wearing a red satin dress. The bride's mother photographed the whole event. There was no music or flowers—just a few of us gathered in the living room, the groom on his knees, looking straight into the three-year-old bride's eyes and promising to wash the dishes for the rest of his life.

The groom was the "bride's" father. Abbey, his daughter, loves to play dress-up. And she adores getting married. It was with all seriousness that she asked us if we would take part in the ceremony. As she recited her vows, she looked as radiant as most real brides we've seen.

One day a five-year-old friend said to us, "I'm not Marcie today. I am the mother of six boys. Let's have coffee and talk." She began to tell us about herself and her children. For the rest of the afternoon, she played at being someone else.

When we were children, many of us used to play dress-up. What a joy it was to delve into those great big boxes of old discarded clothes and in a few minutes be able to transform ourselves into someone totally different. With a bit of creativity and a lot of imagination, we could become anyone we wanted—an Olympic athlete, a movie star, a police officer, or a fairy godmother.

Even without the dress-up clothes, children possess the freedom and flexibility to play at life. Someone once said that the reason we have children is to relive our own childhood. There is some truth in that statement. As we watch our son busily playing with blocks and toy cars and boxes, we wonder how hampered our lives have become by growing out of play. And we think how fortunate we are to have a child, to have an excuse to get down on our knees and roll up our sleeves and build with blocks or race cars across the room.

There is something holy and blessed about playing. It is an act of creating and re-creating, of imagining and envisioning. We don't often think of religious people playing. It seems almost sacrilegious to think about a biblical character or a saint at play. And yet it is just the opposite. It is absolutely proper to associate play with our devotion to God and God's work. A saint in prayer and a child at play are in essence reflections of each other—both suspended in a time and place where all things are possible and for at least a little while one's self is lost in the moment.

King David is a wonderful example of a person who participated in holy play. When King David brought the ark to Jerusalem, he and "all the house of Israel" rejoiced by "dancing before God with all their might, with songs and lyres and harps and tambourines and castanets and cymbals" (2 Sam.

6:5). One can picture David so engaged in the act of frolicsome praise that he didn't even notice his surroundings.

Jesus, too, seemed to be playful. There was a sense of amusement and joy in the air as Jesus told stories instead of delivering lengthy lectures. Jesus artfully crafted words together so that the meaning was shining brightly just below the surface of the parable, so that all who had the ears to hear could discover it.

Perhaps God's creation of the world was the ultimate act of holy play. Perhaps God dreamed and wondered and wished, and then with intense concentration and rolled-up sleeves, God molded and created until God got it right, until God could finally step back and say to the universe, "Yes, this is good."

On our grown-up days—when we work very hard scrubbing our sinks and calling clients, washing clothes and writing reports, changing diapers and merging companies—perhaps our lives could be enriched by some holy play. Sometimes, when we put our work aside for a while and allow ourselves a bit of diversion, God's Spirit visits in new and unexpected ways, and we find insight into our lives. Many writers and other creators talk about how they find inspiration for their work when they play a bit in another medium. Writers may spend time sculpting, and sculptors may dabble at writing.

What would it be like if we approached our prayer time or our Bible time as if it were play time? What if we daydreamed and doodled? What would it be like to draw a picture, write a poem, or compose a song? What if we let loose our spirits and breathed deeply and played just for the sake of playing?

Many people have talked about discovering healing in laughter. Why not introduce some healing, giggle-inducing play time into our daily lives? Some will say it's a silly idea. Then again if God had had colleagues to consult over the creation of the world, they, too, might have said, "Now, God, don't you think that's just a little frivolous? Besides, it will never work." We can be thankful that there were no naysayers. So go for it; play a little today. And as you play, may God's Spirit meet you in your games and bless you.

Questions for Reflection or Discussion

1. What were some of your favorite games as a child?
2. Recall a time when you became so absorbed in what you were doing that you were like a child at play. What was helpful to you in that experience?
3. What forms of play do you find most enjoyable? (Playing can include listening to or playing music, engaging in a physical activity, solving puzzles and word games, writing, or making something with your hands.)

Challenge

Incorporate one of the following playful approaches to prayer into your daily devotions this week (or create one of your own):

1. Listen to inspirational music and dance your prayer.
2. Make a drawing (crayon on paper or chalk on the sidewalk) that expresses to God your gratitude and your hopes.
3. Take a walk in a park or nature preserve. Find a place to sit and reflect, and compose a poem-prayer to God.

7

Cobwebs in the Corner

2 Samuel 11:27–12:15

Our seven-year-old neighbor, Kevin, doesn't think of himself as a prophet. He just tells it the way he sees it. On a visit to our house with his mother, Kevin glanced about our humble dwelling and then declared, "You have cobwebs in the corner. You should get rid of them." His mother blushed and cast him a glance indicating that as soon as they returned home, he would receive a lecture about tactfulness.

Kevin's mother didn't know it, but that wasn't the first time he'd pointed out our housekeeping foibles. The previous summer he informed us that our windows were dirty and that weeds were sprouting up through the cracks in our driveway. "You should pull those," he told us, sounding like a future highway inspector.

Kevin's penchant for audacious observations is probably one of the reasons why he isn't the most popular kid on the block. We appreciate him the way we appreciate the warning lights in our car. We'd rather not see him. When we do, we heed his advice. Though we sometimes find Kevin's remarks annoying, we also know that he speaks the truth. In our busyness we tend to overlook the cobwebs and the weeds that gradually infiltrate our home and property. We grow so used to looking out spattered windows that we fail to realize that we aren't seeing clearly. Much as we hate to admit it, Kevin occasionally helps us to get our lives back in order by pointing out the obvious.

Perhaps Kevin is our neighborhood prophet in the truest sense of the role. Although we sometimes think of prophets as people who are able to predict the future, the actual task of biblical prophets was to clarify the present for those who were overlooking the obvious. God blessed prophets such as Jeremiah, Amos, and Hosea with the ability to clearly see what was wrong with the world and then assigned them the unenviable task of pointing it out to others. It's no wonder that prophets were not popular.

One of the most moving stories about a prophet is the account of Nathan and King David. After David committed adultery with Bathsheba and then arranged for her husband, Uriah, to be killed, God sent Nathan to show the king the error of his ways. Nathan told a parable to David, which helped him to see the grievous crimes he had committed. David responded by repenting of his sins and asking God for mercy. The fact that adultery and murder were displeasing to God should have been obvious to David. Yet in his desire to justify his actions, David had become blind to the truth. It took the bold actions of a prophet to set him straight.

In our modern world, we're not so sure about prophets. At a time when cult leaders have led many astray, we're rightfully wary of people who claim to come bearing a message from God. Still, we look to our teachers and preachers to explain how Jesus can guide our lives. However, that doesn't mean we want them to be prophetic, confusing us with the facts. Many a preacher who has dared to take on the role of truth-teller on

Sunday morning has awakened on Monday without a job. Others face both silence and anger from their parishioners. We might want to be followers of Jesus. That doesn't mean we want anyone telling us the truth about our lives.

Yet from time to time we all encounter people like Kevin—people who are able to see the cobwebs in our lives and aren't afraid to point them out. Often these prophetic types are children, perhaps because they have not yet learned that most people don't like to be told the obvious, especially when it is not the most pleasing news. But others emerge as prophets, too—if only we have ears to hear. Our prophets may be the very old, people way beyond caring about who they might offend. Also, they may be strangers—people who can speak freely without worrying that they may have to confront the issue or the hearer on a day-to-day basis. In moments of courage and wisdom, all of us can serve as prophets. Everyone we encounter in our lives may function as a prophet for us, pointing out the obvious and pushing us to accept the truth.

We may not enjoy Kevin's bold reminders to clean the cobwebs out of the corners and wash our windows. We may even find him annoying. Although we avoid him from time to time, we cannot argue the fact that we need him. Our world needs prophets. We need people who can see through the pomp and circumstance and declare, "The emperor has no clothes." We need people who can point to the spiritual cobwebs in our lives. For as unpleasant as it may be, we need the truth. We need to be able to look in the mirror and see the smudges of dirt on our lives. Only then can we approach God, face-to-face, and ask for forgiveness. Only then can we set out on our journey seeing clearly, knowing who we are, where we have been, and where we are going.

Questions for Reflection or Discussion

1. Who have been the prophets in your life?
2. How have you responded when you were confronted with a truth you didn't want to hear?
3. When have you felt moved to be a prophet to others? What happened?

Challenge

Be your own prophet. Imagine that you need to deliver a prophetic message to yourself.

Make a list of the issues you need to address.

Write out a message, using words that both comfort and challenge.

Put the message in a place that will be helpful to you.

8

Cardboard Castles

Isaiah 40:1–11

A path of brightly colored cardboard bricks stretched from the front door to the fireplace. Lying end to end, they made a long oval shape. Here and there, the builder had added height by piling bricks on top of one another. The oval "castle" (as the five-year-old builder, Alice, had instructed us to call it) was inhabited by a sundry collection of stuffed animals and dolls. At one end of the castle, blond-haired dolls enjoyed afternoon tea in the garden. In the center, a zebra and a hippo rested on an upturned green shoe box, sunning themselves. At the far end of the oval, stuffed rabbits, kittens, and turtles slept silently under washcloth blankets.

This castle community existed peacefully within the house of the human family for many hours until Alice's mother said, "Time to put away your toys."

Immediately, Alice pounded her tightly balled fist on the floor and wailed. "Please don't make me take my castle down," she pleaded. "I'll do anything. I'll even set the table. Just don't make me put it away."

Alice wanted her creation to be permanent. She couldn't comprehend a world that insisted her beautiful castle could not stand forever.

Most of us have a little of Alice in us—maybe more than we want to realize. We want our work to be noticed and remembered. We want the rituals and the relationships in which we participate to last forever. Even as we are wishing and praying for permanence, we know that much of life is like building cardboard castles in the living room. Nothing on this earth can or should last forever.

Life changes with every breath we take. Every day we age, and the bodies we have come to know (even if never to love) seem to deceive us. Illness, death, and natural disasters tear people's worlds apart. Everyone and everything we meet and grow to love on this earth changes and eventually dies. Still, we keep at it. We keep building castles and villages, making love and giving birth, digging in the dirt and reaching for the sky, hoping to create something of substance, if not permanence.

Alice put away her toys that day. The next day she built a village under the dining room table. That, too, had to be taken down. Her apartment building perched on the plant stand, her office beneath the coffee table, and her campsite in front of the fireplace all met the same fate. But Alice kept trying. And her persistence is encouraging. For in the midst of an unstable and difficult world, our small actions of envisioning, loving, and creating are signs of hope. We hope that what we do will make a difference and that no matter what happens, God's love and presence will have permanent places in our lives.

When the people of Israel were exiled to Babylon, they thought it would be temporary, so they didn't want to settle and build their lives there. They hoped to live out of their traveling bags until the time came to move home again. But the prophet Jeremiah instructed them to

> build houses and live in them; plant gardens and eat what they produce. Take wives and have sons and daughters; take wives for your sons, and give your daughters in marriage, that they may bear sons and daughters; multiply there, and do not decrease. But seek the welfare of the city where I have sent you into exile, and pray to God on its behalf, for in its welfare you will find your welfare. (Jer. 29:5–7)

Jeremiah's advice is good for all of us. Life on this earth may be temporary, but in living and loving we will find our welfare.

This lesson hit home during a particularly stressful time in our lives. As we complained to a friend, he scribbled a note on paper and handed it to us. It read: "RX: Cultivate your own garden." In other words, despite life's impermanence, despite feeling alienated, plant what you can. Do not fret over poor soil or insufficient sunlight. Do your best with what God has given to you. Don't worry about the inevitable frost to come. Marvel at the beauty of your flowers while they bloom.

The prophet Isaiah wrote, "The grass withers, the flower fades; but the word of our God will stand forever" (Isa. 40:8). All of us are living a temporary existence. Only God remains a constant. Still, like Alice, we need to keep building castles. Like the exiles, we need to seek the welfare of the place where we are. We need to cultivate our gardens.

Questions for Reflection or Discussion

1. What are some examples of "cardboard castles"?
2. Think about a "cardboard castle" from your past—something you spent a lot of time creating that did not last.
   Which was most meaningful to you: the process of creating it or the finished product?
   Why did you "take it down"?
   What was the experience of "taking it down" like for you?
3. How does "building castles" affect our relationship with God?

Challenge

This meditation reminds us that "life changes with every breath we take." Choose one of the major changes in your life (moving, graduation, the death of a loved one, the end of a relationship). Consider the following questions (you may want to record your reflections in a journal):

1. What did you learn from this experience?
2. In what ways did this experience impact your life?
3. How did your relationship with God affect this experience?
4. What have you learned since this experience that might have helped you at the time?

9

"When I Am Five"

1 Samuel 3:1–18

In a recent conversation with our four-year-old friend, Lily, she revealed to us that she was eagerly looking forward to turning five.

"Why?" we asked.

"Well, there are some things I can't do until I am five," Lily replied quite definitely.

"What things?"

Lily responded with a whole list of activities: "Ride a bike, build a snowman, turn a somersault, climb a tree, cross the street alone, and play an angel in the church play."

We could understand that Lily's parents wouldn't allow her to ride her bicycle or cross the street alone until she reached a certain age. Yet we wondered aloud why she wasn't able to turn a somersault or build a snowman until she turned five.

"I don't know why," Lily answered—and then added with conviction—"I just know that when I am five, I'll be able to do those things and a whole lot more too."

We find both hope and discouragement in Lily's statement. We see hope in such utter confidence that she will be able to do all things wonderful when her next birthday comes around. Still, we are troubled by her assertion, "There are some things I can't do until I am five." Lily's conviction that she is not yet ready to attempt some new accomplishments may be the only obstacle preventing her from achieving them.

Our four-year-old friend isn't so different from most of us. Too many of us put off using the gifts and talents with which God has blessed us, waiting until what we think is the right time, until we feel we have the proper skills or enough money. The thirteen-year-old longs to be sixteen. And the sixteen-year-old longs to be eighteen and then twenty-one, dreaming of all that can be accomplished at the next magical age.

Regardless of our age and amount of talent or experience, many of us seem convinced that we can't accomplish certain tasks until we're older, wiser, and more mature. Even as adults, we remain certain that at some fictional future time we will be more prepared. We pass our days waiting for that opportune moment when life can finally begin. "Oh, I'll be able to do that," we say, "when I get married, earn more money, retire; when the children graduate from diapers, from high school, from college; when it gets warmer; when the television season goes into repeats; when football season ends."

Most often there is not a magical moment when suddenly we feel able to accomplish the heart's desires. Friends of ours recently welcomed their first child into the world, after years of putting it off, hoping for perfect timing. One of them said, "We kept waiting to feel ready. We finally realized that we would never be fully prepared. We couldn't imagine a time when we would have enough money and knowledge to raise a child. And so we took a leap of faith."

In a story in the Hebrew Scriptures, God called out to the boy Samuel in the middle of the night (1 Sam. 3:1–18).

Although Samuel first failed to recognize God's voice, when he finally realized who was calling his name, he responded, "Speak, for your servant is listening." He did not say, "Come back when I am older or wiser or less sleepy." He said, "Speak."

In the Gospels, when Jesus called out, "Follow me," his disciples responded immediately. Simon, Andrew, James, John, and Matthew dropped what they were doing and left their jobs and families to follow Jesus. No questions, no stall tactics, no apparent doubts—just straightforward obedience.

When we first become Christians, God calls each of us to a lifetime of service. God encourages us to serve in ways that make use of our particular blessings and talents. Throughout our lives, God reminds us of this call to serve. God speaks to us, nudges our shoulders, and tugs at our hearts, prodding us at the right moment and toward the appropriate project.

If at this moment we are hearing God's voice, if God's invitation to serve is tugging at our hearts or pushing at our shoulders, then why should we wait another minute? God would not be asking us to serve, to give of our time and our talent, if we were not ready. The time to respond is now—when God's voice is still ringing in our ears.

Questions for Reflection or Discussion

1. God spoke to Samuel in the night. How does God speak to people today?
2. When in your life have you heard God's invitation to serve and answered it? What made it possible for you to say yes?
3. When in your life have you heard God's invitation and not responded? What prevented you from responding?

Challenge

Make a list of one hundred of the tasks, activities, or goals you want to accomplish before you die. You may repeat items on your list.

Which of these tasks or activities is God calling you to start now?

Choose at least one item on your list, map out a plan for reaching your goal, and then take the first step. Do it now!

You may find it helpful to repeat this exercise twice a year.

10

"Read It Again"

Luke 22:7-23

We were delighted when our friends entrusted us with the responsibility of helping their three-year-old son get ready for bed. After we made sure that he had brushed his teeth and washed his face, Noah informed us that he would not go to sleep until we had read his nightly bedtime story.

He chose a favorite book and snuggled beneath the covers. We took turns reading each page of the story aloud while Noah listened intently. Whenever we missed a word, Noah corrected us, revealing that he knew the story by heart. Yet Noah listened with great concentration, as though he were hearing the book for the first time. When we finished the book, our three-year-old friend was still wide awake. "Read it again," he insisted. Since it was a short story and he seemed in no hurry to fall asleep, we read it a second time.

After we finished, Noah stared up at us with his eyes wide open. "I like that story," he said. "Read it again." And so we did—a third time and a fourth. Each time we read the story, Noah appeared to enjoy it just as much as the time before. We read that book through six times before the lights finally went off in Noah's room.

Later that evening, we told Noah's parents how much we had enjoyed reading their son's favorite book. Even though the book was short and simple, each time we read it we noticed something new in the story or illustrations. We sensed that Noah probably did too.

Most children who are Noah's age have a high tolerance for repetition. In fact, by repeating the same activities again and again, they learn and grow in understanding.

The morning after our bedtime experience with Noah, we attended church with his family. Although their congregation is part of a different denomination from the one we attend, we felt at home as we worshiped there. We sang familiar hymns, recited the Prayer of Jesus, and listened to the stories from the Scriptures. As we worshiped that Sunday morning, we realized that like Noah, the people of God deepen their spiritual life through repetition.

Week after week God's people gather for worship, praising God with the words of hymns they first learned as children. Day after day we pray with words we have committed to memory, the same words that Jesus taught his disciples. We read and listen to psalms, parables, and other oft-repeated Bible stories. And though many of us know these hymns, prayers, and scripture passages by heart, we do not tire of them. Each time we say or hear the words, their meaning speaks to us in new and various ways.

Throughout the Scriptures, God's people were commanded to remember all the marvelous things God had done for them. And the people remembered by repeatedly hearing and telling the stories that reveal God's grace. The people of Israel, freed from slavery in Egypt, were commanded to tell the story of their escape from the pharaoh each year at Passover (Exod. 13:3–10). At the Last Supper, Jesus instructed the disciples to eat and drink in remembrance of him (Luke 22:19). Ever since then, Christians have shared in this supper, remembering Jesus and his words.

Learning these stories is like learning to play the piano. We repeat them, catching first the melody—the central characters, the major events. Then we learn the harmony—the sounds and smells, the tastes and sights—that enrich the story for us, bringing Bible times alive. When we are learning the piano, we play the music again and again until it seeps into our night dreams and our daydreams, until the pulsing of the beat becomes part of our very being, as natural to us as breathing. It's the same with the stories. They become a part of who we are. Someone once said that he had read some of his books so many times that he no longer remembered if the stories he carried in his head were truly stories of his family and friends or merely the stories he had read in books.

As we hear these oft-told stories, as we make them our own and then pass them on to our children, our lives are joined together around a common history. Moses becomes part of our family, as do King David and Mary and Jesus. With each new hearing, we become better acquainted with these family members. And the stories of their lives teach us about our lives. The very same God who blessed them is the One who blesses us— week after week, again and again, from cradle to grave.

Questions for Reflection or Discussion

1. What were your favorite childhood stories, and why?
2. What is one of your favorite Bible stories?
3. What stories from your childhood do you enjoy sharing with others?
4. What are some other repetitive actions that you appreciate, and why?

Challenge

Think of three stories from your life that reflect your identity or personality. Record these stories in a journal, and then consider the following questions:

How have these stories shaped the way you think of yourself?

What characteristics about you do they reveal?

If you could edit the stories, how would you change them?

11

Everyone Needs a Cheerleader

1 Thessalonians 5:8–14

It's a simple game, and thirteen-month-old Luke has just figured it out. He grasps a small rubber ball in his hand, crawls across the kitchen floor, and drops it in a wastebasket held by his proud father.

As soon as he has accomplished the task, Luke peers up at his parents and with wide, expectant eyes waits for the response he knows he'll receive. "Yes! Way to go, Luke!" exclaims his father. "Good job, Luke," his mother cheers, clapping her hands. Luke beams as if he has just won an Olympic gold medal. His father pulls the ball out of the basket and hands it to his son, so that he can repeat the performance.

Luke's parents realize that they may appear a bit comical delighting in their son's ability to accomplish a task requiring a minimal amount of motor development. Yet they know that this is just the beginning. In the years ahead, they will continue to play the role of Luke's cheerleaders as he moves on to bigger accomplishments.

Luke probably won't ever win a gold medal or a Nobel Prize, but most likely he will learn to ride a tricycle, then a bicycle, and then to drive a car. He'll need someone to mend his scrapes and scratches when he falls, someone who won't laugh when he tries to parallel park for the first time, someone who will beam with joy and pride when he brings home his driver's license.

His parents know that in the years ahead they may find themselves in humid, overcrowded school auditoriums or wobbly bleachers behind third base, sitting on the edge of their seats, praying that their son will hit all the right notes or that he won't strike out. And Luke will peer up, scanning the crowd with wide, expectant eyes, knowing that whether he succeeds or fails at his latest endeavor, he will hear the voices that have cheered him on since birth, "Way to go, Luke! We're proud of you!"

Not all children are as fortunate as Luke, knowing that someone will always be present to support them. Yet there is a need within all of us, children and adults alike, to know that someone believes in our abilities, loves us unconditionally, and is not afraid to cheer us on. We never lose that need to be praised for what we have accomplished and lifted up when we have failed.

Many successful people write in their memoirs that they couldn't have realized their achievements without someone to cheer them on. Most of us know that to be true. When we finish a project, we look forward to complimentary words from our colleagues and supervisors. After cooking a special meal for family and friends, we wait to see smiles of satisfaction and to hear words of thanks. When we get our hair cut or buy a new outfit, we hope to hear praise from someone. That cheering, that unconditional love and support, provides us with the spiritual anchor we need to feel secure as we venture into the world.

A friend reports that the most moving part of her seminary graduation was emerging from the chapel into a sea of her former teachers, who applauded the achievements of her graduating class. She talks about how that very tangible demonstration of support buoyed her spirits throughout the first weeks of her new pastorate. It reminded her that she had the support of her seminary faculty behind her each time she preached or held the hand of a dying parishioner.

As the Christian community, we need to be cheerleaders for one another, heeding Paul's admonition to "encourage one another and build up each other" (1 Thess. 5:11). Most churches celebrate the big events in their communal life—anniversaries, new pastorates, and building programs. Yet churches also need to recognize and rejoice in the less visible successes—the children who regularly attend church school, the adults who participate in small group ministry, the countless volunteers who keep programs running smoothly week after week.

As families and friends, we gather for birthdays, send cards for marriages and births, and cheer on graduations. Why not also celebrate the completion of a week at work or school, a dinner that turns out right, or even the spring garden planting? When we cheer our friends and family members, we become tangible and audible reminders of God's grace. We provide the Christian support that gives them the courage to be witnesses to Christ in the world.

Questions for Reflection or Discussion

1. Recall a time when being cheered by another was exactly what you needed.
2. In what ways can the members of your family, church, or religious community better serve as cheerleaders to one another?
3. Who have been your cheerleaders? Make a list.

Challenge

Brainstorm a list of people you can cheer on and ways you can do it. Then start cheering!

12

A Sacred Space

Luke 5:15–16

A visit to our house presented four-year-old Kimberly with an afternoon's refuge from her three-month-old twin brothers. As soon as she arrived, we offered to take her to the zoo or to the video arcade. Kimberly shook her head and said, "No thank you. Could I please build a fort instead?"

We agreed, helping Kimberly move chairs into a corner of the dining room. We watched as she draped bedspreads and blankets over the chairs so that her fort was well protected. The shell of the fort completed, she spent the next fifteen minutes furnishing the inside. She dragged sleeping bags and pillows into her fort and arranged them with great care. She then stocked her fort with a few basic necessities—crayons, paper, books, stuffed animals, and snacks. Finally, with a smile, Kimberly announced, "It's finished!"

"Now what?" we asked. "What should we play?"

Kimberly replied, "Would you mind if I just played alone? We have so many people at our house."

The four-year-old spent the rest of the afternoon playing by herself in the fort. Periodically, she emerged for reassurance or refills on food. When her mother arrived to take her home, Kimberly was reluctant to leave. "But I love my fort," she wailed.

Many of us remember the childhood joy of creating a space of our own. The space might have been a tree house, a secret secluded spot in the backyard, or a little-used closet. The space provided a personalized, cozy place to be alone in the midst of a busy household. In that fresh space we felt safe to think new thoughts. From that new vantage point we could retreat into a fantasy world, imagine new possibilities, or simply gain perspective on our lives.

As adults, we may experience similar feelings when we take a retreat or have the opportunity to spend time in a new place by ourselves. The time away—separate from our busy lives and apart from the mounds of stuff we've accumulated—provides a wonderful space in which to imagine, dream, and think.

Many of us build our lives around a work ethic that values what and how much we can produce. Life becomes a treadmill of tasks from which there seems to be no rest. As we become better at our jobs, more tasks are added, and we move faster and faster. We take almost no time out for reflection. And even if we are fortunate to have a space of our own, we often cannot afford the time to enjoy it. Instead our days are spent paying for it, cleaning it, and managing the stuff inside it.

Living on this treadmill of tasks, we do not know how to step off it—even for a brief respite. We may brag or complain about how much we work and how little time we have for ourselves. All the while, somewhere deep inside where none of our friends or colleagues can see, we still have a vision of ourselves as a child sitting cross-legged inside that peaceful fort. Somewhere inside, we still yearn for sacred space, that time alone when we can release our minds from all the duties and stuff of our lives and imagine new possibilities.

When we read the Gospels, we see that our modern lifestyles stand in stark contrast to the way Jesus lived. Many times he worked long hours preaching, teaching, and healing, surrounded by great masses of people. Yet Jesus also made a regular practice of creating time and space to be alone. He retreated to the mountain or to other lonely places to consult God, to nourish his soul, and to find strength to continue his ministry (Matt. 14:23; Mark 1:35; Luke 5:16). Jesus regarded the moments away from the crowds as sacred. And he taught his disciples to pray alone (Matt. 6:6).

We all need sacred spaces. Maybe our lives don't allow us the time to build a fort like Kimberly did. Yet why can't we create a place that can be our sacred space when we need it? We need a place that is free from the demands of work and relationships. We spend much of our adult lives caring and providing for others—spouses, aging parents, children, friends, and clients. Sometimes we need to step away from those who need us, step into the silence, and take time to nourish our hungry souls.

Creating a sacred space, a rest stop for both body and soul, doesn't need to be complicated. We could choose a chair as our quiet spot, making certain that we always use it for prayer and reflection. We may outfit a drawer, a basket, or a box with a journal and a Bible and a book of prayers. Or maybe we can put these things into a backpack and hike to a sacred space outside. And if we can begin with that, with creating our own sacred space, maybe we could consider giving ourselves an hour, a day, or a weekend on retreat. We need uninterrupted time to meditate, connect ourselves to God, and evaluate our lives. We cannot do this while running on our treadmill—juggling tasks, stuff, and relationships. We need a space apart, a place of silence, a sacred space.

Questions for Reflection or Discussion

1. What were some of the sacred spaces in your childhood?

2. Take a few moments to evaluate your current life situation. Rate yourself on a scale of 1 to 10 (1 = "Help! My life is out of control!" and 10 = "I take time each day to nourish my soul"). What can you do to create the sacred space and time you need for spiritual nourishment?

3. If you could plan the perfect spiritual retreat, what would it look like?

4. If you are in a group, share resources for retreats (this might include books, retreat houses, and leaders). If you are alone, check out your library, local church, the Internet, or friends for information.

Challenge

Plan to give yourself a retreat—even if it's just for a day or a morning. Write down some questions you might want to use as a focus for your retreat. Think about a location and a time. If you are going alone, you might want a book to guide your meditation. Be sure to take your Bible and a journal.

13

"Who Do You Love More?"

1 John 4:7–12

We were talking with a friend in her kitchen as she made supper for her two young daughters. Suddenly, our conversation was interrupted by the older daughter, Nora, who came bursting into the kitchen with an urgent question.

"Mommy," she asked, "who do you love more—me or Natalie?"

"Oh, Nora," our friend replied with a gentle smile, "why do you and your sister keep asking that silly question?" She then proceeded to explain that while Nora and Natalie were two distinct persons, both of whom possessed admirable characteristics, she did indeed love both of her daughters equally.

"Yeah, sure," said Nora. "I knew you'd say that. But I can tell that you really love me more because you're making spaghetti for supper and you know that's my favorite."

Nora then rushed out of the kitchen as abruptly as she had entered, shouting at her sister, "Hey, Natalie, Mommy does *too* love me better." No doubt, this argument would continue for a while.

Most children occasionally spar with their siblings or other children, trying to gain the favor of their parents or adults in positions of authority, such as teachers or coaches. This need to be the favored, the first, the best, and the greatest seems to be an innate aspect of human nature. It often begins at home when, like Nora, we vie for the better part of our parents' affection. It continues as our school systems encourage us to compete by bestowing grades and honors upon us, tangible rewards for our efforts. But we don't cease competing when we graduate from school. Our consumption-oriented society urges us to buy bigger, better, and more beautiful products to stay steps ahead of our friends, neighbors, and coworkers.

We once counseled two brothers, both of whom were in their late forties, as they argued with each other about their father's will. In their exchange of insults, we couldn't help noticing that the two middle-aged fellows sounded like a couple of feisty ten-year-olds on the verge of exchanging blows.

The Scriptures contain a number of stories about jealous, squabbling siblings. In one of the most ancient Hebrew tales Cain murdered his brother, Abel, because God "had regard for Abel and his offering, but for Cain and his offering God had no regard" (Gen. 4:4–5). The twins Jacob and Esau emerged from their mother's womb already embroiled in a battle to gain their parents' favor (Gen. 25). A generation later, Jacob's favorite son, Joseph, was sold into slavery by his jealous brothers (Gen. 37).

These ancient stories are about more than dysfunctional families engaged in sibling rivalries. These stories delve into a shadowy aspect of human nature. From earliest childhood, many of us wrestle with the desire to feel superior to others in some way. If our efforts to gain favor are thwarted, jealousy, bitterness, and feelings of inferiority may result.

When we consider that God is the ultimate authority in our lives, the One who relates to us as the perfect, all-knowing Parent, the question, "Who do you love more?" takes on cosmic significance. Many of us want to be assured that God loves us more than God loves our sisters and brothers on this earth. This desire lies at the heart of racism, sexism, nationalism, and denominationalism. At their most basic levels, these institutional evils can be characterized as two children engaged in a petty argument. They wag their tongues at each other and chant inanely, "God loves me more than God loves you. God made me superior to you. God likes the way I do it better than the way you do it."

Bringing racism, nationalism, and the other isms that divide humanity to an end is no simple matter. Yet during his ministry on this earth, Jesus devoted a large portion of his time to challenging the assumption that God loves anyone more than anyone else. He chided the Pharisees for their smug belief that their religious practices were favored by God. As a Jew, he spoke and acted favorably toward Samaritans, longtime enemies of his people. Jesus treated women with a respect that astonished others in his patriarchal culture (John 4:27).

The apostle Paul accurately summarized what Jesus' ministry was all about when he wrote, "There is no longer Jew or Greek, there is no longer slave or free, there is no longer male and female; for all of you are one in Christ Jesus" (Gal. 3:28). In his words and actions Jesus made it clear that the answer to the question, "Who does God love more?" is indeed, "I love you all the same."

Like squabbling children, we may not always want to hear that answer. We may even secretly continue to believe that God plays favorites. It may take some of us a while to finally understand that life is not a competition in which we spar to earn God's favor. God is not the Great Teacher who distributes high grades and certificates of honor to those of us who live right. God loves each of us just as we are. God loves none of us more than the rest. God loves all of us with a generosity we may never fully comprehend.

Questions for Reflection or Discussion

1. If you were Nora's mother, how would you have answered the question, "Who do you love more?"
2. When have you needed to hear that "God loves none of us more than the rest"?
3. In what ways does our society convey the message that we need to be "the favored, the first, the best, and the greatest"?

Challenge

The ancient story of Joseph and his brothers can provide insight into how jealousy, pride, and competition affect human relationships. Unlike many tales of squabbling siblings, this one ends happily. Read this story in Genesis 37:1–47:31. After reading this story, consider the following questions (you may want to write your reflections in a journal):

1. How does Jacob show favor to Joseph over his other sons?
2. How do Joseph's brothers act out their jealousy?
3. What is the role of forgiveness in this story?
4. Does this story offer insights into your life situation? If so, what are they?

14

Ask!

Matthew 7:7–11

Annika's mother winked and laughed at us when we offered to take her daughter to the mall. "You don't know what you're getting into," she warned. "Just remember—you have the right to say no."

At the time, we weren't sure what she meant. When we arrived at the mall, it didn't take long to understand her warnings. "Can we pleeease go to the toy store?" Annika asked with a smile so sweet we would have felt like spoilsports had we refused. After half an hour of admiring dollhouses, we convinced Annika that it was time to move on.

As we passed the food court, she made another innocent request: "All that playing made me thirsty. Can I have a soda? Please?"

Having gulped down a thirty-two-ounce drink, Annika made a logical request: "Can we go to the bathroom now?"

And so the afternoon continued: "Can we ride in the glass elevator?" "Please, let's stop at the bookstore!" "Can we ride in the elevator again?" "Do you think that maybe you might be able to buy me that dollhouse we saw?"

With the latter request we finally learned to say no. "That's all right," Annika replied, "I didn't really think you'd buy it for me. But it doesn't hurt to ask."

An afternoon with Annika was nothing short of exhausting. Still, we enjoyed being with her. We admired her straightforward ability to ask for what she needed or wanted. Perhaps we found her so refreshing because as pastors, we counsel many adults who don't know how to make their needs known. We have discovered that an inability to communicate is at the root of many interpersonal problems.

Over the years we have heard statements like these: "My spouse won't help me with the children," "My friends don't understand me," or "My boss doesn't realize that I'm overworked." When someone brings these complaints to us, we inquire, "Have you asked for what you need?" Frequently, we hear the response, "They ought to know what I need. They should see it! I shouldn't have to ask!"

Only God always knows exactly what we need. God alone can see into the deepest, most secret shadows of our hearts and minds. And yet, even though God knows us better than we know ourselves, God still commands us to ask for what we want. Jesus instructed his followers to "ask," "search," and "knock." He compared God to a parent who will not give a stone to a child who asks for bread or a snake to a child who hungers for fish (Matt. 7:7–11). God may not always give us exactly what we want or think we need. Yet God will hear us and respond to us with both generosity and love.

Asking both God and others for what we want opens the door to honest communication and stronger relationships, as long as we are willing to accept that the response to the request may not always be that for which we hope. Asking helps us to name our needs, increasing our self-awareness and helping us to distinguish true needs from mere desires.

Nevertheless, many of us lack Annika's bold resolve. A friend confessed to us that she is afraid to ask for what she wants for two reasons: "First, I'm afraid my request will be rejected. Second, and worse yet, I'm afraid I'll get exactly what I ask for and I still won't be happy. Then I won't be able to complain. I'll have no one to blame but myself."

Asking means taking responsibility for ourselves. Sometimes this involves feeling vulnerable or risking rejection. Yet ultimately, as Annika reminded us, "it doesn't hurt to ask." What hurts is suffering in silence, keeping our needs to ourselves. Our friends may not always hear us out. However, all of us, even the most lonely among us, have one Friend who is always ready to listen.

> Oh, what peace we often forfeit;
> Oh, what needless pain we bear,
> All because we do not carry
> Everything to God in prayer.
>
> —*Joseph Scriven, "What a Friend We Have in Jesus"*

Questions for Reflection or Discussion

1. What are some of the reasons that people don't ask for what they need?
2. Recall a time when you asked someone for something that you later discovered that you didn't really need or want. How did you feel?
3. When have you asked God for something that you did not receive? How did God provide for you in that situation?

Challenge

How good are you at asking for what you need? Rate yourself on a scale of 1 to 10 (1 = "I wouldn't ask for a life preserver on a sinking ship" and 10 = "If I need it, I ask for it until I get it!"). Here are some questions to guide you:

How frequently do you ask for what you need?

Are there people to whom you are more and less likely to make your needs known?

What pushes you to ask?

What prevents you from asking?

In what ways might asking enrich or better your life?

After reflecting and rating yourself, make a list of what you'd like to ask for. (Some items may be as simple as asking your children to help with housework; others may be more complicated, such as asking your boss for a raise.) Choose one item from your list, and ask for it! If you are feeling bold, you may choose more than one item. (Remember, you may not receive what you ask for!)

15

Teddy Bears and
Diamond Rings

Psalm 63:1–8

From the bathroom, five-year-old Shelby let out a shriek that echoed throughout the house. Immediately, her father came running, fearing the worst. When he arrived, he discovered Shelby standing over the toilet, peering into the bowl, with tears streaking down her cheeks. "Rosie's drowning," she wailed.

Not missing an opportunity to play the hero, Shelby's father reached into the bowl and, grasping Rosie by the hair, pulled her out of the water. Rosie emerged from the mishap unscathed, smiling all the while. Shelby was the one in need of comfort. It was the closest she had ever come to losing Rosie, the twelve-inch-high, purple-haired troll doll who was her constant companion. For the past month Rosie had accompanied Shelby everywhere—to the playground, to the dinner table, to bed.

Many children cling to dolls, teddy bears, blankets, or other favorite objects as sources of security. These furry and fuzzy companions help them to survive the terrors of nighttime, doctor visits, and new situations. As they grow older, most children overcome the need to drag along their favorite objects wherever they go. Yet we've also observed many adults clinging to their own grown-up versions of teddy bears and security blankets.

A lawyer friend of ours won't go anywhere without his lucky tie clip. As far as he is concerned, this simple gift from his mother helped him pass his bar exam and land his first job. Many athletes speak openly about their superstitions—how they always make use of a certain piece of sports equipment or wear a special article of clothing for big events.

Some of us adults rely on habits as sources of security. In anxious times, we might smoke, drink, or nibble on chocolate. Other adults cling to people, clutching their loved ones to themselves, hoping that the relationship will provide refuge from the storms of life. Sometimes our adult security blankets are more sophisticated versions of the toys we clung to as children. For many of us cars, jewelry, and electronic gadgets become more than mere diversions or symbols of success. They function as sources of security—replacements for the One who alone can provide us with the comfort we're seeking.

The problem with many of our sources of comfort is that they cannot last forever. Teddy bears and diamond rings can be lost, stolen, destroyed. Relationships end. When these objects or people become the source of our security, we may find ourselves, like Shelby, shrieking in terror at the prospect of losing them.

It makes perfect sense that both as children and as adults, we seek something to hold on to in the midst of life's uncertainties. Teddy bears and diamond rings may serve legitimate roles in our lives. They may function as tangible reminders of the love and security we experience in our relationships (what the religious have traditionally called symbols or icons). However, these material objects can easily become replacements for love and security (in religious language idols or false gods).

The Hebrew Scriptures are filled with admonitions against idolatry, no doubt because of the human propensity for seeking security in material comforts. We want a tangible god we can touch and hold on to. Yet in the midst of our materialism we humans are also spiritual seekers. We long for what transcends the visible, something eternal, a God who won't get lost or grow old. Like the psalmist, we seek the One who will watch over our "going out and . . . coming in from this time on and forevermore" (Ps. 121:8).

God has promised to be our source of security, the One who will never forsake us. God calls us to let go of the material comforts to which we cling. Through our prayers and meditation, God can become as familiar to us as that old blanket or teddy bear we used to cuddle. God can become our favorite friend, the One we cling to in all situations, the One without whom we cannot survive.

Questions for Reflection or Discussion

1. When you were a child, what were your primary sources of security?

2. Describe a time when you lost something or someone that you valued.

3. What do you think are the most tempting idols for people in today's world?

Challenge

Icons can be defined as tangible reminders of a loving relationship. For example, a wedding band could be an icon representing the love and commitment of marriage. Idols can be defined as replacements for the real relationship. For example, when having the perfect wedding celebration becomes more important than the marriage, the celebration can be seen as an idol.

Make a list of the ten objects, people, or abilities you most fear losing. Reflect on what they mean to you, either in your journal or with a friend.

Why do you fear losing them?

What makes each valuable or special?

Do the items function as icons or idols?

16

Clubs

Mark 2 : 1 5 – 1 7

Eight-year-old Marty announced that he and his friends had started a new club. "It's called the Girls Are Scum Club—GAS for short," he said. "Only boys who promise to hate girls and do everything by the club rules can belong." Marty told us that the rules were mostly a secret, but he could share a few of them with us. "We all wear red on Wednesday, and nobody is allowed to touch a girl, ever," he whispered.

Regardless of age, most of us are members of some sort of club. Generally, clubs ask that their members meet certain requirements before allowing them to join. Maybe it's being able to pay the dues, possessing a certain skill or attribute, or even having the right connections. And once they have joined, members must usually abide by certain rules in order to remain a part of the organization.

Clubs can be helpful resources. They provide a setting for people with common interests or professions to form community. A friend who had just opened a business raved about the local professional club. She said that the club was able to answer business questions and help her form valuable connections. Unfortunately, not all clubs function so benevolently.

Like Marty's GAS Club, many organizations, both formal and informal, define themselves not only in terms of whom they let in, but also in terms of whom they exclude. One's gender, race, or other unalterable attributes can keep one out of the group. Often, this results in the emergence of competing clubs that attract those who have been excluded. We weren't surprised when Marty's younger sister informed us that she was in the process of organizing her own special society—the BAD Club (Boys Are Dumb). She hadn't drawn up any rules yet, but we suspect that being a girl would be a definite prerequisite.

Many of us take pride in belonging to a club. It means that in one way or another we are deemed worthy by others. We have been allowed to become part of an elite circle. And it's painful to be left on the outside, to desire to belong to a group and then to be turned away. From the earliest days of childhood, most of us have experienced the turmoil of rejection in one form or another: "You're not good enough for the team," "You don't fit in," or "Sorry, we voted you down." It is not surprising that gangs, which are essentially clubs with guns, often attract those who are marginalized in our society. Being part of a gang can give one a sense of power and belonging in a world where so many are excluded.

In Jesus' day, many people followed laws and commandments that excluded others. Devout Jews could not associate with anyone who was considered to be unclean—people with leprosy, some women, and Gentiles. Devout Jew though he was, Jesus chose to ignore these rules. He healed everyone who approached him with faith, unclean women and Gentiles included. He dined with sinners and tax collectors (Mark 2:15–17). He embraced those outcasts whom the rest of society shunned. Jesus loved and welcomed all people—and in doing so set forth a new, more inclusive vision of community.

The Christian concept of community is based on Jesus' radical inclusion of outsiders. We become community around the One who has brought us new life—Jesus, our Savior. Unfortunately, too many Christian churches function like the exclusive, competing clubs of our childhood. For some, Christian community seems to equal agreement or consensus. They may gather together because they like to revel in their sameness. Or they unite around pointing to the sins of others. Those who accept the consensus of the group belong; those who define themselves differently are excluded.

These club-churches are not really Christian. Jesus said, "Love your neighbor as yourself." He didn't say, "Love the neighbors who are *like* yourself." Jesus isn't present when two or three gather to exclude or condemn or hate. One of our seminary professors said that whenever we draw a circle and say that "Jesus is with us and not with those of you on the outside," chances are good that Jesus is with the outsiders.

The apostle Paul echoed Jesus' understanding of community when he exhorted the Christians in Rome to "welcome one another, therefore, just as Christ has welcomed you, for the glory of God" (Rom. 15:7). For Paul, and for Jesus, membership in the community of faith was open to all, regardless of qualifications.

As Christians, we are united in Jesus' name. We belong to Christ's church not because of our own attributes or achievements. We belong to God and to one another because Christ has claimed us, all of us, as his own. Jesus asks that we follow him, that we follow his example of loving God wholeheartedly and loving others indiscriminately. Jesus asks that as we gather and form communities in his name, we do so with arms that are open to all, creating a rich and colorful tapestry of people.

Questions for Reflection or Discussion

1. Reflect on a personal experience of "failing to make the club." What was that like?

2. What are some of the most meaningful organizations or groups to which you have belonged? What has made (or makes) them important to you?

3. Who are the people you most fear including in your crowd, and why?

4. Who are the people you most fear will exclude you, and why?

Challenge

Worship or attend a social function in a religious community or church with which you do not ordinarily associate. Reflect on the experience with a friend or in your journal.

Did you feel more or less accepted than you expected to be?

What did you learn about yourself from the experience?

17

If Only

Matthew 28:16–20

Justin seemed to be an ordinary teenager. Like many people his age, he enjoyed living in the moment—whether it was spending time with his girlfriend, working on his car, or cruising Main Street in the small town where he lived. Although his graduation day was just a year away, Justin spent little time considering his future. After high school, he figured he would get a job working on an assembly line at the local factory. In the meantime, he just wanted to have a little fun.

Then, in an instant, Justin's life changed in a way he had never imagined. While driving alone on an icy winter night, his car skidded out of control and crashed into a tree. Somehow, Justin survived the accident. However, he soon learned that his spinal cord had been damaged and that he would probably never walk again.

As he lay paralyzed in a hospital bed for many months, Justin gradually realized the ways in which his life would no longer be the same. His legs, once lithe and strong, had withered like limbs on a dying tree. He could no longer control the simplest bodily functions. And worst of all, Justin's girlfriend announced that she couldn't deal with the accident and was leaving him. In his lonelier moments, Justin blamed himself for the accident, considering what he could have done to prevent it. "If only I'd stayed home that night," he would say. "If only I hadn't been driving so fast."

In the midst of his depression Justin was surrounded by family and friends who prayed for him and encouraged him not to lose hope. And somehow, over time, Justin's attitude began to change. He thought seriously about his future. Instead of longing to return to his past, he realized that before the accident, his life had been quite aimless. Throughout the next year, as he worked with counselors and therapists, Justin started to set goals for his life. Members of his church raised money to buy him a new car, which he could drive without use of his legs. Justin received his high school diploma, applied to college, and made plans to start his own business.

Whether we are one or ninety-one, we all experience crises in our lives. Sometimes we face them and move on. Other times we dwell on the pain and difficulty. We may become stuck on one distressing event and use that experience as an excuse for wallowing in self-pity. We may say that we could have done wonderful things with our lives—"if only." If only we had listened to the warnings. If only we hadn't become ill. If only we could have some control over life's random acts of misfortune. If only God would bless us with a neatly packaged solution.

The disciples must have felt that way after Jesus' death. When Jesus was arrested and crucified, they were caught completely by surprise. They acted lost and forsaken. Peter denied Jesus and then broke down in tears. Mary wept by the tomb. The disciples huddled together out of fear of the religious authorities. No doubt, their talk must have been littered with the paralyzing phrase "if only." If only Jesus could have lived. If only he hadn't offended people. If only Judas hadn't handed him over. If only we had come to his defense. If only the religious authorities hadn't killed him.

Through the resurrection, God turned the crisis of Jesus' death into a new opportunity. When Jesus was resurrected, he went to his disciples, giving them a vision to follow. He instructed them about their future ministry. Jesus challenged them to look ahead and move forward instead of dwelling on the past. And so, when Jesus ascended and sent the Holy Spirit, the disciples were no longer lost. They had a vision, a mission, and a ministry. There was not time to sit and ponder "if only." There was work to be done.

Vision is the key to freeing us from becoming stuck in the crises that we all encounter. Justin's vision of a new life freed him from his depression. Jesus' commission of the disciples to ministry provided them with the vision they needed to move forward. And with vision, we, too, can unlock our hopes and dreams and move on.

St. James's Church in Piccadilly Circus, London, has this sentence written on its mission plan: *A vision without a task is a dream, a task without a vision is drudgery, a vision and a task is the hope of the world.* We need the marriage of vision and task to move on. When the two meet and we begin the journey forward, guided by God, we find freedom from dwelling in the past. We no longer need to linger on what would have happened "if only."

Questions for Reflection or Discussion

1. Recall an inspirational individual who has faced a crisis and moved beyond it. How has his or her story given you hope for your life?

2. How have difficult experiences brought blessings to you in the past?

3. What have been your visions and how have you needed to modify them as you have experienced various circumstances in your life?

Challenge

Reflect on the following questions in your journal:

What events or experiences in your past are you having difficulty letting go of and moving beyond?

What would need to happen so that you can let go and move on?

Write a plan of action for at least one event or experience, and begin moving forward!

18

Temper Tantrum

Mark 11:12–25

It has been an enjoyable evening of game playing and conversation. Perhaps too enjoyable. For now that bedtime has arrived, Hannah doesn't want the evening to end. "No! Let me stay up!" she shouts when her father tells her to change into her pajamas.

Hannah's father calmly explains that play time is now over and that four-year-olds need to go to bed at an earlier hour than adults. "No!" Hannah wails as her mother takes her by the hand and guides her toward the bathroom. Suddenly, Hannah breaks free of her mother's grasp and plunges facedown onto the floor, shrieking and flailing as if she has been thrown into a vat of boiling water.

"You hate me!" she shouts in a fit of heartfelt overacting.

When her father responds by stating that no, her parents do not hate her, Hannah changes her approach. "Well, I hate you!" she howls, now doing her best imitation of a demon-possessed maniac who has lost all control of her senses.

Of course, the child is not possessed by demons. She doesn't really hate her parents, and she knows they don't hate her.

She is exhausted and frustrated, that's all. Hannah's parents carry her to bed, kicking and screaming. They help her say her prayers, give her a goodnight hug, and then leave her to sob herself to sleep. In the morning she'll wake, refreshed and cheerful, her bedtime temper tantrum a distant memory.

It's a familiar event for anyone who has been around children. In the preschool years, when most children have not yet learned the inhibitions that restrain them from openly expressing their anger, temper tantrums are especially common. Many times these public displays of rage are the result of pure frustration; other times they are tests to see how much the child can get away with.

Few adults would want to emulate Hannah's fit of rage. Most of us are aware of the hazards of expressing anger inappropriately. Yet Hannah's temper tantrums can teach us something about what it means to live in a trusting relationship. Hannah feels free to express her anger because she knows that her parents love her. She feels loved enough to scream the things she fears the most—that her parents really do hate her, that they secretly wish she had never been born. When we can utter those words, it usually means we trust that others will continue to love us in spite of the horrible things we think or say or do. It means that the relationship is strong enough to survive an occasional bout of anger or doubt or fear.

We all get angry from time to time. We've all had people angry with us. Unfortunately, in many popular religious circles, Christians are encouraged to stifle all anger. Jesus is remembered as the passive and mild-mannered Child of God who never so much as raised his voice.

Yet when we turn to the Scriptures, we see that Jesus sometimes expressed feelings that we may try to suppress, including anger and doubt. Just after Jesus' triumphant entry into

Jerusalem, he cursed the fig tree. While confronting people who were using the Temple grounds to make money, Jesus became ferociously angry, overturning tables and pouring out the coins of the money changers in a sort of "Temple tantrum." In the Garden of Gethsemane, Jesus did not hesitate to express his real feelings; he told God exactly how he felt and even asked to have the cup removed from his hands. Jesus did not act the part of the ever cheerful Child of God with a plastic smile plastered on his face. Jesus was truly human, fully experiencing and expressing pain, anger, and doubt.

As such, Jesus is a role model for us in our relationship with God. Many of us would prefer that God see only our good side—the side we show to acquaintances and distant relatives who occasionally drop in for a visit. We want God to come into our lives when the house is clean, the children are well behaved, and we are dressed in our Sunday best. We want God to see us acting kindly toward others, reading our Bibles, and remembering to tithe. And so when we feel angry and disenchanted and frustrated, we take it out on ourselves, our families, our friends, sometimes even strangers. We don't include God in our tirades.

And yet God, who loves us like a perfect parent, with an unconditional, forgiving love, can handle our anger. God knows us through and through and, even so, will never desert us. We can trust this love. Indeed, we can trust God even more than we can trust ourselves. God wants us to trust enough to say what we feel at all times. God, who loves us without restraint, wants us to be secure enough in this love to invite God to be a participant in all of life—the better and the worse.

Questions for Reflection or Discussion

1. In what ways do you express your anger?
2. What do you consider to be inappropriate and appropriate ways of expressing anger?
3. Recall a time when you felt angry with God. How did you express that anger?

Challenge

Think about a time in your life when you struggled with anger. What do you wish you had said to God?

Write a psalm or prayer of anger to God. (For inspiration, read Psalms 13, 22, and 35.)

19

Her Brother's Speaker

Matthew 7:1–5

Like many twins, five-year-olds Nate and Kate spent much of their time together. They shared a number of interests, although their personalities were markedly different. Nate was the quiet one who never spoke unless he had to. Kate was outgoing and sometimes a bit domineering.

The twins' mother observed that as a result of their different personalities, Kate had become her brother's "spokesperson." Once in the midst of a violent thunderstorm, Kate ran to her mother and reported, "Nate is scared. We better go comfort him."

On another occasion Kate declared that "Nate doesn't like carrots. Maybe we shouldn't have them for supper anymore."

One day Kate announced, "Nate would like to get a rabbit for a pet." Since the twins' mother knew that her son had long hoped to become the owner of a puppy, she asked him directly if what his sister had reported was true.

"No," he replied softly. "I want a puppy. *She* wants a rabbit."

Further discussions with Nate revealed that carrots were actually one of his favorite vegetables and that he wasn't afraid of thunderstorms. And so during the next storm, when Kate came running to her mother and said, "Nate's afraid," her mother knew what to do.

She held out her arms and replied, "Kate, it's all right for *you* to be afraid. Do you want me to hold you?"

Suddenly, a streak of lightning lit up the darkened house. Kate rushed into her mother's grasp. As the thunder roared, Kate trembled. As the raindrops pattered against the windowpanes, tears poured down Kate's face. A few minutes later, Nate wandered into the room and said, "This storm is the best. Hey, what's wrong with Kate?"

Even a beginning psychology student could diagnose what was wrong with Kate. Sigmund Freud was one of the first to give her condition a name—"projection." *The American Heritage Dictionary of the English Language* defines this term as "the naive or unconscious attribution of one's own feelings, attitudes or desires to others." Children often project their needs or feelings onto others, even their stuffed animals, making statements such as, "Teddy needs a drink of water."

Projection isn't something we grow out of, like sneakers or thumb sucking. A friend who is a therapist told us that her clients frequently say, "I'd like to save the marriage, but my spouse refuses to change." Inevitably, investigation of the situation reveals that the one making that statement is usually the one who is most unwilling to make changes in the marriage.

We have spoken with pastors who, when challenged to try a new approach to ministry, announce flatly, "Oh, the members of my church would never go for that." Since it's impossible to ascertain the opinions of several hundred church members without consulting any of them, we suspect that these pastors may be projecting onto their parishioners their own unwillingness to consider new ideas.

On the surface, projection may seem to be relatively harmless. On a deeper level, it can be the source of hypocrisy. Sometimes we are less tolerant of people whose particular shortcomings mirror our own. When we are unwilling or unable to face our own problems directly, we may begin to attack others. As in sports and war, we may be inclined to act on the principle that the best defense is a good offense. If we dwell on other people's problems, we feel less need to attend to our own. However, when we acknowledge and resolve a problem in our own lives, we are often better able to help others with similar problems. Support groups such as Alcoholics Anonymous are built on this principle.

Long before the advent of modern psychology, Jesus recognized the human tendency to project our sins onto others. "Why," he asked, "do you see the speck in your neighbor's eye, but do not notice the log in your own eye?" (Matt. 7:3). Jesus' solution to the problem of projection was simple: "First take the log out of your own eye, and then you will see clearly to take the speck out of your neighbor's eye" (Matt. 7:5).

The congregations we serve practice the ritual of corporate confession. Before we sing the opening hymn, we take a moment to silently examine our lives. We consider the ways in which we have disappointed God. We think about the good we have failed to do. In essence, we take a moment to remove the logs from our eyes. We pray that God will provide us with the ability to be loving in all we say and do. And then we listen to God's words of forgiveness. We hear the swoosh of the eraser over the chalkboard of our lives. The slate is clean. We can start again.

This ritual of confession and forgiveness provides us with the opportunity to look honestly at our lives. We need that time each week, even every day. We cannot look inwardly when we are worrying and wondering about what others are doing wrong. When we finally stop fretting about the shortcomings and problems of others and look into our own hearts, we become aware of our hurts and needs. Then we can open ourselves up to the healing forgiveness of God. Then, like Kate, we can welcome the comforting hug of another. We can allow God to embrace us and heal us.

Questions for Reflection or Discussion

1. In what ways might have Kate's projection of her own feelings onto Nate prevented her from receiving what she needed?
2. Why do you think so many people have difficulty taking responsibility for their own feelings?
3. Consider some problems you have worked through in your life. How has your experience enabled you to help others who confront similar problems?

Challenge

Set aside time for individual confession and forgiveness. Find a quiet place where you can be alone for a while.

Begin by reading Psalm 51. Scholars believe that this psalm was written by King David as a confession after he committed adultery with Bathsheba and arranged to have her husband, Uriah, killed (see 2 Sam. 11–12).

Take time to reflect on some of the ways in which you feel that you have failed God. (Think hard if you have to!)

You may choose to record some of your reflections with chalk on a child's chalkboard or with pencil on a piece of paper.

Reread Psalm 51:10–12 while erasing what you have written.

As a reminder of God's forgiveness, read Psalm 103:8–12. You may want to record these verses in ink on paper and post them where they will be an ongoing reminder of God's compassion for you.

20

"Stop Fussing and Enjoy the Scenery"

Numbers 21:4–9

At least twice a year one of our friends, a single mother of two daughters, packs her children and what seems like most of their belongings into their station wagon. After checking to make sure that everyone has been to the bathroom and loading three bags of snacks, they begin the two-hundred-mile drive to Grandma's house. Ten-year-old Susan has been on the trip enough times to know that the drive can be agonizingly long. And so on a recent trip, when her younger sister asked an inevitable question, Susan was ready with the answer.

"Mommy, are we almost there?" asked six-year-old Marin after half an hour on the road.

"Shh," replied Susan. "Don't bother Mom. We'll get there when we get there."

"But this is taking forever," whined Marin. "How much longer?"

"Shh," replied Susan again. "Now stop fussing and enjoy the scenery."

No doubt, a two-hundred-mile trip in the car can seem like an eternity to a six-year-old. Yet young children are not the only ones who hate to wait. It's been said that we live in a "quick fix" society. If we feel hungry, most of us can pop a meal into the microwave or head to our nearest fast-food restaurant. In a matter of minutes we can consume enough calories to last the rest of the day. If we are short on cash, we can stop at an automatic teller machine and in seconds have enough money to buy an entire wardrobe. And if all else fails, we can usually take out a plastic card and buy whatever we think we need on credit.

In our goal-oriented culture, if we aren't immediately satisfied, we join young Marin's plea, "How much longer?" But we certainly aren't the first human beings on this earth to whine about just how long it takes to arrive at our destination. The ancient Israelites, freed from slavery, journeyed in the wilderness to the promised land. The journey took an unexpectedly long chunk of time, forty years. Even in that slower-paced society, forty years was a long time. In fact, for some, it was a lifetime.

The Israelites certainly let God (and Moses) know of their dissatisfaction. They kvetched and complained, moaned and groaned, even reminisced about the "good ol' days" when they toiled as slaves in Egypt. We wonder what they were missing while they were complaining. Did they notice the extraordinary sunsets, spread all pink and red across the evening desert sky? Did they relish the feel of hot sand between their toes? Did they look around in amazement at God's gift of manna, food in a barren land? Or were they too focused on getting to the end of their journey to enjoy the process?

In our modern impatience, in our desire for fulfillment, we, too, sometimes miss seeing the gifts of the journey. Big sister

Susan advised Marin to stop fussing and enjoy the scenery. How many of us, impatient to get going and get on with it, need to hear Susan's advice? We feel so busy and divided as we juggle responsibilities at work and home that we do not stop for even a moment to breathe and acknowledge life's daily blessings.

A popular magazine featured an article on time management for busy women. It encouraged the reader to get more accomplished each day by doing two or three tasks at once. "Don't just cook dinner," the article advised, "do squats while you slice vegetables." And so those of us who are already six years behind on our to-do lists feel chastised because we can't manage to complete enough tasks! We certainly aren't coordinated enough to master squats and vegetable cutting without a major catastrophe.

Perhaps it's time to throw away that article and listen to Susan: "Stop fussing and enjoy the scenery." Stop complaining about how long it takes to get to work or how the kids are whining again or how the only meal you have time to eat is one of those frozen microwavable dinners. Instead, look around and count your blessings. Enjoy what you can see when you are driving slower. Listen to what the children are actually saying. Thank God for the gifted wizard who created frozen dinners for you to heat and eat.

At this time, in this moment, in the here and now, we possess only the present and all of its joys and sorrows. God has given to us the *present* as a *gift*. When we stand in the present and look around at all we have, piled before us like gifts beneath the Christmas tree, and we stop saying, "But I didn't get everything I wanted," and instead we look to God and say thank you, we begin to experience the gift of contentment. We remember how very blessed we are.

Our friend has told us that the family's trips have become much more bearable since Susan has taught Marin how to enjoy the scenery. On a recent trip, she reported hearing Susan say to Marin, "If you lean back and stare out the windows at the sky, you can see the clouds. And each cloud can be a face. Hey, there's Goldilocks. What do you see, Marin?"

Questions for Reflection or Discussion

1. What are some of the times in your life that you need to hear Susan's words, "Stop fussing and enjoy the scenery"?
2. At what times in your life do you most crave a "quick fix," and why?
3. Think about your life as a car trip and consider these questions:

   At what times have you been primarily focused on reaching your destination?

   When did you enjoy the process of traveling?

Challenge

Choose a task that you would prefer to hurry through or combine with other chores (for example, cooking, grocery shopping, commuting, or doing yard work). This week, pay attention to the experience of completing the task. Do not combine it with other chores or activities. Try to focus exclusively on the task at hand. Then consider the following questions (you may want to write your reflections in a journal):

What are the aspects of the task that you find enjoyable?

What most bothers you about the task?

How could you make the experience more pleasant?

Did paying attention to this task change your experience of it? If so, how?

21

Night Terrors

Mark 4 : 3 5 – 4 1

Six-year-old Matt was haunted by night terrors. Every night he feared falling asleep. He suspected that monsters and ghosts hid under his bed. Most nights he woke up screaming. When one of his parents comforted him, Matt reported that three-headed monsters or child-eating dinosaurs had come out from under the bed and chased him.

His parents tried every manner of cure. They explained to Matt that the monsters were merely the creation of his extremely active imagination. When he refused to believe them, his parents taught him to imagine himself chasing the monsters away. But Matt said it never worked. The monsters always found a way to surprise him, to turn the tables on him and attack. Then he tried confessing his fears to six miniature "worry dolls," which he placed on his bedside table. The hand-made figures were supposed to hold all of Matt's troubles until morning, leaving his mind free for pleasant dreams. Still the night terrors continued.

Finally, Matt's parents found a tactic that worked. Every night before bedtime they lay on the floor and shouted into the space under the bed, "Monsters, goblins, ghosts, and ghouls, be gone. We banish you from Matt's room." They would begin and end the rite with a prayer, asking God to protect him and grant him a peaceful night's rest. Gradually over a period of weeks, Matt's night terrors became less frequent. And then his fears of going to sleep subsided as well.

Matt's experience brings to mind Jesus' words: "Peace I leave with you; My peace I give to you; not as the world gives, do I give to you. Let not your heart be troubled, nor let it be fearful" (John 14:27 NASB). When Matt was experiencing night terrors, it occurred to us that we all are in need of some comfort. Many of us adults are troubled by fears as well—terrors that sneak out from the shadows of our lives. Like the monsters beneath Matt's bed, our fears often attack us when we are feeling most vulnerable—in quiet moments when we are alone, when the noise and clutter of life's daily distractions have abated. We may fear being abandoned, or we may fear being smothered by those we love. Some of us fear failure; others fear success. Many of us fear being unattractive, getting sick, growing old, and dying.

Like Matt and his parents, we seek all manner of cure to help us banish our fears. We race through our lives frantically searching for something to fill the aching dread within our souls. We buy self-improvement books to help us name our fears. We take sleeping pills and painkillers to relieve our suffering. We buy clothes and cars and computers, we dye our hair blond and black and red, we fall in and out of love, we gorge on double cheeseburgers and chocolate fudge sundaes, and with all of this we try desperately in every moment to forget that the fears exist. We look to all this stuff to fill us up so that we won't feel our spiritual hunger. We long for peace.

We want someone who cares about us to hold us tight and tell us it's safe, we're okay, we're loved. What we really need is Jesus.

Jesus has promised us that he will give us peace—peace that we will not find on this earth. He says the world just cannot provide this sort of peace. Searching the world for peace is like asking a cow to give you eggs. Not possible. Jesus has promised to give us this peace so that we can banish our fears and calm our troubled hearts. It's as if Jesus is promising to come into the room at night, get down on the floor with the dustballs, look under the bed, and say, "Fears, be gone. I banish you from this life." It's as if Jesus is saying he'll be there each night to pull the covers up over us, tuck in our fingers and toes, and wait with us until our troubled hearts find rest. And Jesus can do this for us. He will. Fears, be gone. Jesus is here.

Questions for Reflection or Discussion

1. What fears haunted you as a child? What fears haunt you now?
2. What rituals helped you to overcome your childhood fears? How do you try to banish your fears today?
3. Describe a time when you were afraid and someone helped you find peace.

Challenge

Make a commitment to set aside time to meditate this week. As you meditate, imagine Jesus coming into your life and helping you to banish your fears. It may help to recite John 14:27 and listen to soft instrumental music. Afterward, reflect on this exercise in a journal.

22

Imaginary Friend

John 20:19–29

We were paying a pastoral visit to one of our parishioners, the mother of a five-year-old girl named Anna. As we talked in the living room, Anna played quietly by herself in her bedroom.

"Will she be okay?" we asked.

Anna's mother pointed to the well-worn baby monitor. "She knows to call if she needs me. And we'll hear any emergency," she said.

A few minutes into our conversation, Anna began to talk, as if to a friend. We paused for a moment so that we could hear her words in case something was wrong.

"Now, Jesus," said Anna, "you sit here in this blue chair, and I'll sit in the red one. Would you like some lemonade? I know it's your favorite drink. I'm so glad you could come over today. I needed to tell you some things."

Anna's mother turned down the volume on the monitor. She blushed as she explained to us that Anna had taken to heart a church school lesson in which she learned that Jesus is always with us.

"Since then," said Anna's mother, "Anna talks about Jesus being here almost every day. Jesus eats all his meals with us. And, of course, he likes to get out and walk with us in the evening. I even had to move a sleeping bag into Anna's room so that Jesus would have a comfortable place to sleep at night. I guess you could call Jesus her imaginary friend."

Anna's mother paused and then peered at us nervously. "Uh, I guess that doesn't sound quite right. I mean as Christians, we believe that Jesus is real, don't we?"

We agreed with Anna's mother. It did seem odd to refer to Jesus as Anna's imaginary friend. The word "imaginary" suggests that Jesus is a pretend or fantasy friend, someone quite unreal. Later, it occurred to us that perhaps a better word for Anna's friend Jesus would be "imagined."

When we imagine, we create in our minds an image of something that is not currently present to us and our senses. That does not mean it is unreal. On hot, hazy days in late summer we might imagine a gentle breeze, a cooling rain, even an icicle, in order to feel more comfortable. When we imagine, we can also create images that are beyond our realm of experience. Most of us in our early teen years, long before we had experienced true love, imagined romance and created images of falling in love.

In a similar way, Anna imagined Jesus. She had never met Jesus face-to-face in what we understand to be *chronos* or "clock time." So Anna created for herself an image of the very real Jesus. The relationship we had witnessed between Anna and her imagined friend Jesus sounded remarkably like the picture of faith put forth by the writer of the letter to the Hebrews: "Now faith is the assurance of things hoped for, the conviction of things not seen" (Heb. 11:1).

In the best sense of the word, Jesus was Anna's "imagined" friend. Jesus was not her "fantasy" or "pretend" friend. For even though she had never seen him or touched him, by faith Anna experienced that Jesus was really present with her, just as many other Christians do. Anna's experience is not so different from what Christians do week after week as they gather to worship or celebrate Holy Communion. Theologians speak about the "real presence" of Christ. Many Christians draw comfort from Jesus' promise that "where two or three are gathered in my name, I am there among them" (Matt. 18:20).

Worship, prayer, and listening to scripture are all acts of profound imagination in which we open ourselves to the presence of God in our midst, an experience that transcends our senses. In the Gospel story about Thomas, the disciple remembered as the doubter, Jesus praised the faithful who believe without ever seeing: "Blessed are those who have not seen and yet have come to believe" (John 20:29). In the Gospel of John, Jesus spoke at length about the Spirit of truth (or "the Advocate") who enabled Jesus' followers to imagine Jesus' ongoing presence in their lives, even after Jesus had left them: "This is the Spirit of truth, whom the world cannot receive, because it neither sees nor knows this Spirit. But you know the Spirit, who dwells with you, and will be in you" (John 14:17). Contemporary Christians continue to speak of the Holy Spirit as an unseen yet real power who guides and inspires the faithful.

In the years we have served as pastors, we have observed that children are often more able to accept the elements of the Christian faith that require an active imagination. Every Christmas we struggle to answer a host full of children's questions about the events of Jesus' birth: What does a manger look like? What kinds of animals were there? What were the names of the angels who appeared to the shepherds? No doubt, the children asking these questions are able to envision the events described in the Christmas story with a clarity and a depth that have long since eluded us adults.

For children (and willing adults) imagination is a powerful force. And for this reason, it can also be a source of danger. We noticed that Anna served Jesus a glass of lemonade because it is his "favorite drink." Actually, lemonade is Anna's beverage of choice. Herein lies the danger—in our imagining we are prone to envision Jesus in our own image, to create a God who is nothing more than a shadow of ourselves, a God who looks, acts, and thinks just like we do.

Although the ability to imagine Jesus' presence can bring comfort in the midst of life's more difficult moments, we must also be willing to acknowledge the limits of our imagination. No single image can contain the One we call Christ; no single vision of God's presence is adequate. Perhaps that is why Jesus used some unlikely images to describe his presence in this world—as a stranger, a prisoner, and a person in need (Matt. 25:31–46).

In time, we hope that Anna will come to know Jesus as more than a friend who drinks lemonade and camps out on her bedroom floor. As she grows in years, we hope that she will continue to be active in a community of faith where she will learn from other Christians whose imaginations challenge her to experience Christ's presence in ways that stretch beyond her life's boundaries and open her eyes to new possibilities. For now, we think she is quite fortunate to have such a wonderful imagined friend.

Questions for Reflection or Discussion

1. If you were Anna's mother, how would you respond to her having Jesus as her imaginary friend?
2. How did you use your imagination as a child?
3. What are some ways that people cast Jesus in their own image?

Challenge

On a day that you are at home, preferably alone, follow Anna's example and let Jesus be your imagined friend. Talk aloud to him; give him a seat at your table; make room for him wherever you are.

Later, take time to reflect on this experience. You may want to record your thoughts in your journal. Use the following questions as a guide:

Did you feel uncomfortable imagining Jesus? Why or why not?

Did you tend to envision Jesus in your "own image"? How?

What did this experience teach you about your relationship with Jesus?

23

Whose Fault Is It Anyway?

John 9:1–12

Accidents happen. And this one was just waiting to happen. Our friend's antique vase, a family treasure, sat precariously on top of the mantle in her living room. She had intended to move it to a safer location while her grandsons, ages ten and eight, visited for a week. But as she anxiously prepared for their arrival, the antique vase slipped her mind.

On the second day of their visit, she remembered it, exactly at the moment she heard the unmistakable sound of glass shattering against a hardwood floor. As she stepped into the living room to survey the damage, her usually boisterous grandsons peered up at her in awkward silence. Then before she had a chance to ask any questions, Cal, the ten-year-old, pointed to his brother and said, "Doug did it."

"What do you mean?" Doug retorted. "You're the one who threw the ball."

While the two brothers tried to pin the blame on each other, their grandmother carefully picked up the pieces of her broken treasure, quietly chiding herself. *If only I had remembered to move the vase . . .*

Misfortunes befall us. Shortly after her parents divorced, seven-year-old Felicia walked into her pastor's office with tears rolling down her cheeks. "God doesn't love me anymore," she said.

"Why do you think that?" asked the pastor.

"Because I'm bad. I'm grumpy to my mommy and I'm nasty to my daddy and I'm mean to my brother. That's why Daddy doesn't live with us anymore."

The pastor assured her that she was not responsible for her parents' divorce, but Felicia continued to sob. "I promise to be good," she wailed. "If I'm good, will God make Daddy come back?"

When accidents happen and misfortunes befall us, we often ask, "Who's responsible?" When things go wrong, some of us, like Felicia, blame ourselves. Some of us, like Cal and Doug, try to pin the blame on others. And some of us decide that God must be responsible.

Perhaps this desire to find someone to blame for our problems relates to a basic human need to be in control of our lives. If only we can isolate the reasons for life's difficulties, then we can determine our own destinies.

Children often utilize what psychologists call "magical thinking." Magical thinking is the belief that our thoughts and actions have the power to control life around us, including the behavior of others. Felicia blamed her parents' divorce on her own conduct. Therefore, she believed that if she could change her behavior, if she could be good, then she could prevent her parents from divorcing. Felicia learned that she has no such power. Sometimes there's nothing we can do to prevent life's disappointments.

Our desire to make sense of life's random misfortunes may drive us to create scapegoats. Especially in moments of great anxiety, we may seek out someone to blame. The Salem witch trials and the mass extermination of entire groups of people remind us of the tragic consequences of blaming gone hysterical.

Our need to know "who's responsible" is not a new one. In John's Gospel, the disciples asked Jesus, "Rabbi, who sinned, this man or his parents, that he was born blind?" Jesus responded, "Neither this man nor his parents sinned; he was born blind so that God's works might be revealed in him" (John 9:2–3).

The disciples' question pointed to their faulty thinking. In asking, "Who sinned?" they wanted to blame the man or his parents for the man's blindness. According to Jesus, it was not appropriate to ask who sinned or who bore the responsibility for the man's blindness. No one can answer that question. Still, said Jesus, God's power can be revealed through the man's situation. And God's power was revealed when Jesus healed the man.

As we encounter life's difficulties, we may be tempted to apply magical thinking—to believe that our bad behavior causes God to make bad things happen to us and our good behavior causes God to bless us. When we cannot blame God or ourselves, we may seek to make a scapegoat of others so that life will make sense.

Unfortunately, every aspect of our lives doesn't make sense. The world doesn't always operate by linear principles. We cannot consistently pinpoint a cause for every experience. Sometimes accidents happen, and there is no logical explanation.

Still, in the midst of life's mysterious difficulties, Jesus reminds us that God remains ever present. Jesus challenges us to move beyond our magical thinking and our need to create scapegoats. Jesus invites us to fully experience God's presence and power in all of life's moments, even when the circumstances of those times disappoint us.

92.....whose fault is it anyway?

Questions for Reflection or Discussion

1. If you were Felicia's pastor, how would you respond to her question, "If I'm good, will God make Daddy come back?"
2. What are examples of scapegoating besides the ones mentioned in the meditation?
3. Reflect on times when you have blamed yourself for events that were beyond your control. What are some alternative ways you could have understood the situations?

Challenge

Read chapter 9 of John's Gospel. Jesus said, "Neither this man nor his parents sinned; he was born blind so that God's works might be revealed in him" (John 9:2–3). How do you think "God's works" were revealed in this man?

Reflect on an especially difficult time in your life. Consider the following questions (you may want to reflect on these questions with a trusted friend or in your journal):

Who were you tempted to (or did you) blame for your situation?

If you did blame, did it help or hinder your process of working through a difficult time?

How were God's works revealed in the situation?

Looking back, how would you handle the situation differently?

24

Mimics

Ephesians 4:31–5:2

Strolling through the neighborhood, we overhear two children engaged in a game that only one of them wants to play.

"Leave me alone, Julie," says the boy.

"Leave me alone, Julie," replies his sister with a tone of derision in her voice.

"I mean it. Stop repeating me," he says.

"I mean it. Stop repeating me," comes the echo.

And so the game proceeds, until one of the participants becomes angry or uninterested and finally puts an end to it.

As we continue our walk down the street, we pass a teenage couple holding hands. He sports a Green Bay Packers jersey bearing the name and number of one of the team's star players. She self-consciously tosses back her hair, which is styled in the same manner as the latest supermodel gracing the pages of this week's fashion magazines.

At the end of the block we stop to watch a pickup game of basketball. "Hey, look at me," shouts a slightly overweight five-foot-two-inch pale-faced boy with pimples. "I'm Michael Jordan." He leaps as high as his legs will lift him, releases the ball in midair, and watches as it drops with a perfect swish through the hoop. It's quiet in our neighborhood, but that young boy hears eighteen thousand voices in his head, cheering on their hero in his moment of glory.

These children and teenagers are mimics, all of them, continuing a pattern of behavior they first learned as infants. By mimicking, they learned to walk and talk, hold a spoon, read a book, and dribble a basketball. And if they're like most people, they'll continue to be mimics for the rest of their lives, even long after they've abandoned their dream of gracing the cover of *Vogue* or *Sports Illustrated*.

The word "mimic," which literally means "to copy or imitate closely," originates from the Greek *mimikos*. It is the word that Paul used when he wrote, "Therefore be *imitators* of God, as beloved children, and live in love, as Christ loved us" (Eph. 5:1, emphasis added). Paul no doubt recognized children's proficiency at mimicking. And since Christians relate to God much like children relate to their parents, Paul encouraged Christians to imitate Christ.

Mimicking Christ is both the same as and different from the game we played as children. At one level, it is simple imitation. The most basic thing that Christ has done for us is to love us. Paul was saying to imitate this about Christ. Live in love. Love God and love one another. In the most straightforward terms, that is what it means to be imitators of Christ.

At another level, imitating Christ means living a life that reflects God. We are created in God's image. Our person and our actions reflect our Creator. Usually, when a child is born, many hours are spent discussing the child's resemblance to family members. As children grow, we begin to see in them reflections of their ancestors. "Oh, she has her mother's smile," we say. Or perhaps, "He talks just the way his grandfather did." It's the same with our faith life. The hope is that when people look at us, they catch a glimpse of our Creator. Maybe it's in how we speak kindly of others. Or the way we welcome strangers into our homes. Or the love we provide our children. Or perhaps it's just something in our eyes, something that says, "I'm a child of God."

The leader of a Bible study group in which we were participants asked our group to list the characteristics we shared with Jesus. We felt daunted, comparing ourselves with the Savior. Then as we talked together and looked at the Scriptures, a whole list of Jesus' gifts emerged. We began to list them—patience, compassion, hospitality, faithfulness, and more. In time, we saw the ways in which we were imitators of Christ.

Still deeper, imitating Christ means taking his message and making it our own. We might be copying the bold strokes of Jesus' life when we love others as he first loved us. But the details—the colors, the style, the form—are all our own. As Christians, we need to move beyond rote imitation, beyond the game of mimicking, and into a lifestyle in which we mirror Jesus in our own unique ways.

Questions for Reflection or Discussion

1. When you were a child or a teenager, who were the people you imitated?
2. Who are your role models today?
3. In what ways are you a role model for others?

Challenge

Make a list of some of the characteristics you share with Jesus.

Reflect for a moment on the following questions:

How in your life have you made these characteristics your own?

How do you use these gifts to minister to others?

Choose a concrete activity that makes use of some of these characteristics, and carry it out this week. (For example, if one of your gifts is an ability to teach, consider helping children with their homework at your local library or after-school program.) Be creative!

25

"You Can't Rush These Things"

Luke 18:1–8

Andrew delighted in the special gift he received on his sixth birthday—his own tool set. The gift included a miniature screwdriver, a tiny hand saw that really worked, and a hammer that fit perfectly into a six-year-old's hands. After receiving precise instructions about when, where, and how to use his tools, Andrew spent the next weeks diligently putting them to the test.

He sawed twigs off the lilac bush, pounded nails into scrap wood, and even built a "house" for his sister's dolls. His parents were amazed at Andrew's ability to pass countless hours working on a single task. However, his concentration was disrupted the day four workers arrived to remove a dying oak tree from the family's front yard.

Andrew watched from his bedroom window as the workers used chain saws to take down the tree limb by limb. Within a few hours only a stump remained where the tree once stood.

"Why did they leave the stump?" Andrew asked his mother.

She explained that the tree had roots that spread deep into the ground. The workers needed special equipment to pull up the stump. They would return late in the summer to complete this task.

One morning, several weeks after the tree had been cut down, Andrew's mother observed him squatting near the stump. His hand moved back and forth in a steady rhythm as he sawed at the base of the stump. Andrew remained there until he came into the house for lunch. His mother asked him if he was now working for the tree removal service.

"That's right," he replied as he wolfed down a sandwich. "Those workers aren't coming back. So I'll have to move the stump myself."

Since Andrew's latest obsession was keeping him out of trouble, his mother merely smiled at his earnestness. She didn't bother to tell him that using a miniature saw to remove a tree stump several feet in diameter from its roots was an impossible task.

That afternoon Andrew returned to his work, breaking only for an occasional glass of lemonade. Neighbors passed by and smiled at him. Some even waved. The sunny day grew hot. He kept at his work, seemingly oblivious to passersby, the midday sun, and the aching muscles in his wrist. At midafternoon, Andrew's mother found him resting in front of the television. "All done with your work?" she asked.

"Just taking a break," he replied. And then with all sincerity he added, "Mom, you can't rush these things."

In the following weeks Andrew spent at least an hour every day chipping away at the stump. Finally, one afternoon just a few days before school was to start, Andrew rushed into the house shouting, "Mom! Dad! I did it! I moved the stump."

When Andrew's parents followed him into the yard, they witnessed an amazing sight. Equipped with only a miniature hand saw, their six-year-old son had removed the stump completely from its roots. Andrew's feat will not be recorded in any world record books. Yet his perseverance inspires anyone who feels overwhelmed by a seemingly insurmountable task.

Throughout the Scriptures, God's faithful people practiced perseverance as a spiritual discipline. They heard God's call, plunged forward in faith, and endured in the midst of adversity. The Israelites pressed on toward the promised land despite poor attitudes, a paltry diet, and a difficult journey. Many of the prophets continued to preach despite disbelief, hostility, and danger. Jesus' disciples, bereft after the loss of their leader and confused by Jesus' resurrection and ascension, continued to meet together for prayer and mutual support. All of those people practiced the spiritual discipline of perseverance. Despite the enormity of the tasks before them, the force of the resistance against them, and even their own sometimes poor attitudes, they persevered. And as they worked toward their tasks, they relied on God and their community for support.

The writer of Hebrews, after citing the examples of many personalities in the Hebrew Scriptures, declared, "Let us also lay aside every weight and the sin that clings so closely, and let us run with perseverance the race that is set before us" (Heb. 12:1). God calls us to persevere like the people of Israel, the prophets, the disciples, and Andrew. Those who do heed Andrew's advice (and encouragement): "You can't rush these things." Whether one is building a house, writing a book, or seeking to overcome an addiction, the road to success involves many small steps taken day by day.

Questions for Reflection or Discussion

1. When have you needed to hear Andrew's advice, "You can't rush these things"?
2. What obstacles prevent you from persevering in the tasks you hope to accomplish?
3. Recall a time when God helped you to persevere. What lesson did you learn from this experience?

Challenge

Experts claim that it takes twenty-one days of repeating an activity to turn it into a habit. Set aside fifteen to thirty minutes a day for the next three weeks (twenty-one days) to meditate and pray. Be patient. Remember, "you can't rush these things." At first your mind may drift. You may worry over your to-do list or notice dust on the tables. Here are some techniques to help you:

1. Play soothing music while you meditate.
2. Choose a familiar hymn, scripture verse, or prayer to use as a sort of mantra. It can focus your mind as you meditate.
3. Use an icon or candle to focus your eyes while you pray.
4. Set aside part of your time for free prayer. You may choose to write these prayers in a journal.
5. If you have trouble concentrating inside, map out a fifteen- to thirty-minute walk. Wear headphones with soothing music if you live in the city. Say your prayers or mantra in time to your steps.
6. If you miss a day, don't worry. Just extend your total commitment by one day and start again tomorrow!

26

"I Wish It Could Be My Birthday Forever"

Mark 9:2–8

In a week she would turn three. It was the first birthday that Emily was old enough to look forward to and help plan. Every day when she woke up, Emily would ask her mother, "Is it today? Is today my birthday?" When her mother said no, they would look at the calendar and count the days until Emily's birthday.

After what must have seemed like an eternity to a soon-to-be three-year-old, Emily's "big day" finally arrived. Early in the morning of her birthday, Emily's parents woke her, singing "Happy Birthday." Emily and her mother enjoyed a special grown-up birthday lunch at a restaurant. In the afternoon, family and friends came over for cake and games and gifts. Late that night, after saying prayers and telling stories, Emily confessed to her mother, "I wish it could be my birthday forever."

The Gospels tell the story of Peter, James, John, and Jesus going up to the mountain. And there something wondrous happened. Elijah and Moses appeared to them. Jesus became transfigured before them—changed so that his clothes shone dazzling white, "such as no one on earth could bleach them" (Mark 9:3). A cloud appeared, and from that cloud a voice spoke, "This is my Child, the Beloved; listen to him!" (Mark 9:7). The text tells us that Peter and the others were terrified. We can imagine that they were in awe and felt both uncomfortable and blessed. Peter had no idea what to do at a transfiguration. And so he made an offer: "Let us build three dwellings, one for you, one for Moses, and one for Elijah" (Mark 9:5).

Peter did not want to move on. He seemed to want to stay there, to bask in Jesus' glory, and to avoid suffering. It's as if Peter was saying, "If only this moment could last, then life would be okay, then I would always know where I am and who Jesus is. Then I would feel forever blessed." But of course, Jesus and the disciples could not stay. They had to go back down the mountain; they had to face the future and eventually Jesus' death on the cross.

To some extent, Emily and Peter speak for all of us. We love celebrations. We love those moments when life and our place in it are clear and beautiful and pleasant. Sometimes we wish that we could pitch a tent on one day in our lives and just stay there. We'd like to curl up and eat comfort food forever. But that's not reality. Real life is more like a salad than straight comfort food. Real life is a colorful mix of joy and pain and excitement and downright boredom, all tossed together. Each bite brings new tastes and surprises. Each bite teaches us something about who God is and how God loves us.

And so the real lesson is this: Jesus meets us at all the moments of life—ordinary as well as extraordinary. Jesus is with us when we are on the mountaintop. And he stands by our side when we are down on regular ground, experiencing worry or apathy or restlessness. When we celebrate a new life or an anniversary, Jesus is there, rejoicing with us. But Jesus is also present when we are feeding an infant in the cold dark early morning hours or hauling out the weekly trash. Jesus promises to bless all of life—the daily grind as well as the celebration.

We need to value living in all of life's moments, savoring each one as God's precious gift to us. We often marvel at a child's ability to be present in play and to rejoice over the most ordinary events of daily life. At the age of two, our son, Samuel, did a little dance, a sort of jig, at the mention of something he enjoyed, be it ordinary or special—eating graham crackers, going to his grandparents' house, or reading a favorite book. Samuel's joy over all of life's pleasures helps us to realize that each act in our lives, every moment we breathe, is holy. We don't need to spend our lives wishing and waiting for the grand and glorious moments. For even now, even this ordinary today, can be a joyful, jig-inducing time of celebration.

Questions for Reflection or Discussion

1. What are some of the moments in your life that you wish could have lasted forever? To what future moments or experiences do you look forward?

2. How does remembering or anticipating these times help you in the present?

3. How has God met you in both your mountaintop moments and your everyday life?

Challenge

Make a list of the ten most significant events in your life.

How many were pleasant experiences?

How many were difficult moments?

How many were a mixture of difficulty and pleasure?

Reflect on how you experienced God's presence in all of the events you listed.

27

Hiding Baby Jamie

Mark 14:32–42

Five-year-old Jordan had been a big brother for just two months. When we saw them at church, his parents said, "Jordan seems to be adjusting to baby Jamie." His grandparents exclaimed, "Why, I think he might actually like having a little sister!" On a few occasions we observed big brother Jordan helping his mother push the baby in the stroller. However, Jordan's parents soon recounted to us an episode that revealed that their son wasn't getting used to his sister at all.

One morning, Jordan's mother left baby Jamie in her bouncy seat while she went to answer the phone. Jordan, who had been watching television, carefully lifted Jamie out of the seat and placed her in a laundry basket full of dirty clothes. Then he took some of the dirty clothes and covered her. Satisfied that he had done a proper job of hiding his sister, Jordan sat down and continued watching his favorite show. When Jordan's mother returned and saw that the baby was missing, she inquired, "What happened to Jamie?"

"She's gone," replied Jordan. "She didn't like it here anymore."

"Now, Jordan," shouted his mother, "you know she couldn't walk out the door alone. Where is she?"

Jordan shrugged his shoulders. "I don't know," he lied. "She was here the last time I looked."

Just then baby Jamie wailed and kicked at the denim shirt draped over her legs. Jordan's mother rescued baby Jamie from the laundry basket. Then she sat Jordan down for a long talk.

"Why on earth did you do that to your sister?" she asked.

"I wanted her to go away. I want you to play with just me again," confessed Jordan.

Developmental psychologists have observed that before infants reach a certain age, they lack the ability to discern "object constancy." Infants are unable to understand that when an object is removed from their field of vision, it continues to exist. Only what they can see is perceived to be real.

Since most children grasp the concept of object constancy long before they turn five, Jordan obviously wasn't fooling either himself or his mother. Though he might have wished that making his sister disappear could be as easy as pushing a remote control button, he must have known that his desperate plot to rid himself of his trouble would not be successful. That didn't stop him from trying, however.

Many adults have childhood memories of trying to dispose of their problems by placing them out of sight. "Forgotten" homework assignments. Brussels sprouts slipped beneath the tablecloth. The broken pieces of Mom's favorite dish hidden in a closet where she'll never think to look.

The practice of sweeping the proverbial dust under the rug continues well into adulthood. In many and various ways we seek to avoid our problems, placing them out of sight and mind, as though simply neglecting them could somehow make them vanish. The "dust under the rug" may include broken relationships, worries about our health, our mortality, or discussions we should have had with our spouses, children, or friends. Many of us rely on addictive behaviors such as alcoholism or working excessively to avoid painful aspects of our lives that we would rather not acknowledge. These avoidance techniques are about as effective as turning up the volume on the radio to drown out the rattling sound coming from beneath the hood of the car. Few of life's problems disappear simply because we ignore them.

Perhaps the temptation to place our troubles out of sight is an intrinsic aspect of being human. Even Jesus, in the moments before his arrest, wrestled with the desire to have his problems go away. His well-known prayer in the Garden of Gethsemane, "Abba, for you all things are possible; remove this cup from me" (Mark 14:36), was the heartfelt plea of a man seeking to avoid his mortality. Despite his request, Jesus succeeded where most of us fail. Jesus' resounding conclusion to his prayer in Gethsemane, "Yet, not what I want, but what you want," reveals our Savior's willingness to face life's most difficult challenge.

In our own ways, with God's help, each of us can learn to confront the problems we're tempted to avoid. Though we may be able to conceal our problems from our colleagues, our closest friends, even ourselves, before God "no creature is hidden" (Heb. 4:13). Because God is by nature all-knowing and forever present, God knows the contents of our shadowiest closets and the deepest recesses of our hearts. God knows about the neglected homework assignments, the hidden Brussels sprouts, and the broken pieces of Mom's favorite dish. Sometimes the very act of prayer can help us take the dramatic first step of seeing our lives the way God sees them and acknowledging that our problems exist.

We're not sure whether or not Jordan talked to God about his problem. He does seem to be coming to terms with it. A few weeks after the laundry basket incident, we spoke to him at his sister's baptism. "I guess we have to keep the baby," he announced. Then out of earshot of his mother, Jordan whispered, "Jamie's not too bad. Once you get used to her."

Questions for Reflection or Discussion

1. Recall a time from your childhood when you tried to make a problem disappear by avoiding it or ignoring it. What happened? What did you learn from the experience?
2. In what types of situations are you currently tempted to "sweep problems under the rug"?
3. How does Jesus' prayer in Gethsemane, "Not what I want, but what you want," inspire you when you are tempted to avoid problems?

Challenge

Make a list of things about your life that you try to conceal from other people. (Be honest—if you are human, there are aspects of your life that you try to hide.)

Now use your imagination. Try to look at your life from God's perspective. Everything on the list is known to God, even if it is hidden from others. Imagine what God might say to you about what you keep hidden. Write a dialogue between God and yourself about these issues. Set aside five to ten minutes to do this. (Do not think too much. Just write what comes into your head.)

Afterward, reflect upon what this exercise has taught you.

28

It's Not Fair!

Luke 15:11–32

Our friends' two sons, David and Joey, had just returned from a night of neighborhood trick-or-treating. They sat sprawled on the living room floor, candy spread out in front of them, counting and comparing their riches.

"I got six chocolate bars," boasted David.

"Well, I got seven packs of gum," replied Joey.

"Hey look," shouted David, "I got a squirt gun with five cylinders for water!"

"Where's mine?" squealed Joey, searching through the remains in his bag.

"Ha! You didn't get one," taunted David.

"It's not fair. I got this stupid plastic car. Can I have your water gun?"

"No way. You've got plenty of candy and that car. I call no trading."

David and Joey exchanged more words. As we watched the ensuing argument, we couldn't help observing that Joey had been content with all his Halloween loot until he started comparing what he had with his brother. Comparisons often result in discontentment.

Early in life, most children discover that much in this world is not fair. Beauty, health, and wealth are not doled out in equal measure to all. Teachers, coaches, and even parents play favorites. Studies reveal that in the classroom and on sports teams, certain children are treated more favorably than others on the basis of their gender, race, socioeconomic status, and physical appearance.

In addition, many children learn to compare themselves to others when parents or teachers make comments such as, "Why can't you be more like Johnny or Susie?" As we grow into adulthood, we do not cease this comparing. We check to see how our friends are doing in their careers. We look out the windows to see which new "grown-up toys" the neighbors have recently purchased.

Life seems most unfair when we compare ourselves to others. It always will. At every age, we will find colleagues and friends who have accomplished more and earned more than we have. And we will uncover the discrepancies. Some of our colleagues have been given better opportunities and more valuable advice. They have benefited from advantages that we have not received. Certainly, these injustices ought not be overlooked. And yet even the most vocal civil rights leaders recognize that before one can strive for a more just society, one must first acknowledge and celebrate one's own gifts and blessings. Sometimes we spend so much time envying the good fortune of our friends and neighbors that we fully miss the fact that our own Halloween bag is overflowing with treats.

Jesus told a story that speaks to this. In the parable of the prodigal son (Luke 15:11–32), the younger of two brothers asks for and receives his half of his father's estate. In short order this son squanders all that his father gives him. After wandering hungry and working as a hired hand, he returns to his father. The father, filled with joy over his son's return, throws a huge welcoming party. The older son, who had faithfully remained by his father's side all the while, sees his father doting on his brother and cries, "Unfair!" The father responds, "Son, you are always with me, and all that is mine is yours" (15:31). It is as if the father is saying, "Open your eyes, kid. Look around at the blessings I give you each day."

Like Joey and the prodigal son's brother, we often become most dissatisfied with our lives when we compare ourselves to others. At a Bible study on the topic of gratitude, one of our parishioners shared a story that reminded us of this point. He had recently been turned down for a promotion at work while one of his colleagues with less experience had received a raise. As he sat down at the supper table, he complained in a loud voice about the unfairness of his work situation. Then without thinking, he reached across the table, grabbed a piece of bread, and stuffed it in his mouth. His three-year-old daughter stared at him with a bewildered frown. "Daddy," she said, "you forgot. First we bow our heads."

Embarrassed by his daughter's comment, the man realized that he had become so obsessed with his unfair treatment at work that he had neglected to observe his family's nightly ritual of thanking God for all their blessings before eating supper. "Now whenever I feel like complaining because this world is so unfair, I remember my daughter's comment," he told us. "Before I complain, I bow my head. It makes a difference, you know."

Questions for Reflection or Discussion

1. Who are some of the people you competed with or compared yourself to as a child? In what ways did that affect your self-image?
2. What are some ways that people typically respond when their experiences are unfair?
3. What are some of the blessings you have overlooked in the last week?
4. What do you need to do to become more aware of the blessings that surround you?

Challenge

Some of the most conservative Jews take saying thank you so seriously that they literally pray their thanks for everything they see during a day. And so, upon rising they might say, "Blessed are you, O God, Sovereign of the universe, for you have blessed us with this new day." By the end of the day, they have uttered their thanks for literally thousands of blessings.

Choose a half hour sometime early in the day to practice thanking God for all that you see and experience. You could do this at home, while commuting to work, or on your daily walk.

Later in the day, reflect on how this activity affected your attitude throughout the day. (Who knows, maybe you'll decide to do this *every* morning?)

29

Body Language

1 Corinthians 6:12–20

On preschool picture day, fifty squirming children waited in line in the church basement with their moms, dads, and baby-sitters. Four-year-old Molly tugged on her baby-sitter's arm and whispered, "Mrs. MacDougal, I gotta go potty."

"Can you wait a few minutes, honey? It's almost our turn."

Molly waited. The line moved slowly. Some of the children glared solemnly at the camera even when the photographer's assistant held up puppets to make them laugh. Others threw tantrums about sitting on the hard stool. Minutes passed like hours.

"Please, Mrs. MacDougal," pleaded Molly, "can I go to the potty now?"

"Sweetie, I cannot let you go alone. And there are only two people ahead of us. If we go now, we will lose our turn and have to wait another hour."

Molly jumped from foot to foot, trying to hold it in, looking a little like an Irish folk dancer.

Finally, it was Molly's turn for pictures. She plopped on the stool. As Mrs. MacDougal arranged Molly's red velvet dress, someone started to wash dishes in the church kitchen. Molly held her hands over her ears, but the sound of running water overwhelmed her. Right there on the picture stool, in front of everyone, Molly lost the battle with her bladder.

Children are born with a great awareness of their physical needs. Infants scream and cry when they are hungry, tired, wet, or even lonely. A nutritionist once advised us, "Don't worry about whether every meal your toddler eats is nutritionally complete. Over the course of a few days, he will naturally seek out a balanced diet."

As children grow, however, they gradually learn that their needs—both physical and emotional—cannot always be attended to immediately. The adult world, crammed tight with busy schedules and demanding deadlines, sometimes causes us to ignore important messages from our bodies. Many of us no longer recognize the body's signals for hunger or fullness. Instead of eating to satisfy hunger, we eat to fill our emotional needs. Or we refuse to eat even when we are hungry, hoping to gain control over a small part of our lives. We may know that we need to relax or sleep, but we postpone this much-needed rest until after our work is finished. We may experience physical signs of stress—such as headaches or stomach distress—yet ignore the message the body is trying to send us.

A friend of ours, recovering from a heart attack, confessed that he had been feeling tired for months. He had become obsessed with trying to earn a significant job promotion, working seventy to eighty hours a week while neglecting his family and sleeping just a few hours each night. "I don't want to say that God caused my heart attack," he said. "But I do think God is trying to tell me something. I need to get my priorities straight."

We dwell inside earthly flesh, living in a created world. God formed us this way—to feel pleasure and fitness and love as well as hunger and exhaustion and pain. The psalmist wrote, "For it was you [God] who formed my inward parts; you knit me together in my mother's womb" (Ps. 139:13). Because God gave us these bodies as a gift, it only makes sense that God would communicate with us through our bodies.

The incarnation, the fact that in the person of Jesus God became human, reminds us of the value God places upon our physical nature. If God did not highly regard the human body, God certainly would not have become *one with us.*

Throughout the Gospels, Jesus is described as attending to his physical needs. When he grew hungry, he ate. When he became tired, he rested. And he extended his gifts to attend to the physical needs of others—making withered bodies whole, feeding thousands on a hilltop, changing water into wine.

In his letters to the Corinthian church, Paul frequently wrote about the body, for example, "Do you not know that your body is the temple of the Holy Spirit within you, which you have from God, and that you are not your own? For you were bought with a price; therefore glorify God in your body" (1 Cor. 6:19–20).

Just as we take better care of a friend's vacation home than we do our own homes, we treat our bodies differently when we recognize that they belong to God. When we take the time to attend to our bodies, *our temples of the Holy Spirit,* they tell us what we need to know. Molly's "accident" prompts us to listen to our bodies and care for them, remembering always that we are "fearfully and wonderfully made" (Ps. 139:14).

Questions for Reflection or Discussion

1. Are you more likely to ignore your physical needs or emotional needs?
2. Reflect on a time when you listened to your gut feeling and it helped you.
3. Reflect on a time when you got into trouble because you ignored a physical need or gut feeling.

Challenge

Pay close attention to your physical needs for a whole day. Record them in a journal.

Reflect on how you respond to them. In what ways do you try to ignore your needs? How do you listen to them? What is your body telling you?

Based on this reflection, how would you like to do things differently?

(It may be helpful to do this exercise over several days and in different situations. You may benefit from monitoring how you respond to your physical and emotional needs with friends and at work as well as at home.)

30

Seeing the World Anew

Luke 2:1–20

It was the Sunday after Christmas, our first Christmas as parents, and we were visiting in a new city. We packed our ten-month-old son, Samuel, into his stroller and trekked to a church in the neighborhood where we were staying.

Aware that a ten-month-old child can be a worship disturbance, we peered hesitantly into the sanctuary and sat down in the last row of pews. A moment later we were joined by a young man who smiled and handed us a bulletin. He wore pressed white jeans and a baggy shirt. His hands, bone-thin, stuck out of his shirt like those skeleton hands you see attached to Halloween costumes. His chalky white skin was marked by bruises on his forehead, similar to the marks we have seen on other people suffering from AIDS.

When Samuel began to babble during the service, a number of people turned and smiled at our son, who returned their attention with a grin of his own. The man seated next to us was particularly fascinated with Samuel.

"My name is Christopher. Welcome to our church," he said, leaning toward us and shaking our hands. "You have a beautiful child," he whispered. "Thank you," we replied politely in unison, acknowledging both the welcome and the compliment.

As we sang the Christmas hymn "What Child Is This?" Christopher smiled and wiggled his thumb at Samuel, who was squirming restlessly on his mother's lap. Samuel giggled with delight and reached for the man's hand. With his tiny fists he grabbed the gnarled thumb and held on tight. Then to our surprise, Samuel, who was usually reserved around strangers, crawled out of his mother's lap and into the waiting arms of Christopher.

Before we fully realized what had happened, Christopher was handing baby Samuel back to his mother and apologizing, "So sorry. I know you don't want a sick man holding your baby."

Immediately, we assured Christopher that we didn't mind. He could hold Samuel all he wanted. "Oh, no," we said, "we're not bothered, not at all."

But our assurances came too late. No doubt Christopher had noticed an expression on one or both of our faces, an unspoken gesture, a pulling away, an unconscious apprehensive look. We had done something that betrayed what we were thinking, even while trying with all our might not to think it. A man with AIDS is holding our baby.

As we discussed the incident later, we confessed that while we were trying to remain open-minded, when we met Christopher we both made the same initial observation: This man is sick. When we first looked at Christopher, we didn't see a brother in Christ, a child of God, or another traveler on the road of life. We saw a man with a deadly virus. And although we knew that sitting with this man, embracing this man, even sharing bread and wine with him at the communion table could not pass his illness on to us or our son, what we first saw when we looked at Christopher had built a barrier between him and us.

Then we thought about Samuel. What did he see when he looked at Christopher? From his reaction it appeared that Samuel saw a man with a friendly smile and a very funny thumb. Clearly, at the age of ten months Samuel saw the situation quite differently from the way we did as adults. He had not yet learned to make some of the judgments that we make. As a relative newcomer to life on this planet, Samuel simply marveled and delighted in what he saw—a man who could make him laugh.

One of the greatest pleasures we have discovered as parents is learning to see the world anew through the eyes of a young child. When we watched Samuel's eyes grow wide the first time he stepped outside into a yard covered with snow, we also gasped at the wonder of it all, at least for a fleeting moment.

How delightful (and yes, also vulnerable) it must be to observe the world and all its inhabitants without the discriminating judgments we learn to make as we grow older and more experienced. To see snow without thinking, *It'll take an hour to shovel it.* To meet a man like Christopher without holding back, without thinking, *He's sick; I'd better not get too close.* Just to see the wonder of God's creation and God's many people in all their varied splendor.

Perhaps that is why in the person of Jesus, God chose to enter this world as an infant. Not because infants are necessarily more innocent than the rest of us but because of the sense of wonder and attentiveness with which they regard the world. Perhaps God who is eternal, old beyond our imagining, wanted to marvel at the creation anew and realized that the best way to do that would be through the eyes of a newborn.

And because of that experience, because God once peered out at this world with the vision of a child, even now God continues to see the creation anew each day. God sees each of us—young and old, healthy and sick—as though looking at us all for the very first time, beholding works of wonder and beauty.

Questions for Reflection or Discussion

1. How has your view of the world changed throughout the different stages of your life?
2. Recall a time when you felt that you saw the world in a new way. What was that experience like for you?
3. What does it mean to you that every day God sees you "as though looking at you for the very first time, beholding a work of wonder and beauty"?

Challenge

Spend some time with a child between the ages of six months and five years old with the intention of trying to see the world through a child's eyes. If there are no children in your immediate family or neighborhood, you may want to volunteer at your church nursery, a local library, or a community hospital. Your role is to be a student, allowing the child to teach you about what he or she sees. Sit at the child's level, and play his or her games. Allow the child to lead the conversation. Later, reflect in your journal or with a friend about how your view of the world was affected by this experience.

31

The Faithful Servant

John 6:1–14

Kenny was born with Down syndrome. When we met him, he was fifteen years old and had the mental age of a six-year-old. He attended high school and worked at a center for developmentally disabled people. He had a girlfriend. And he was one of the pillars of the church.

Every Sunday Kenny sat at a table in the narthex and greeted people as they came for worship. Those of us who knew Kenny well could see the hope in his eyes—he wanted to carry the cross in the weekly procession. If he could have done it every week, he would have. Instead, he had to wait until his name came up in the regular rotation. Fortunately for Kenny, many of the other teenage cross-bearers were not as dedicated. And when they forgot to show up, he was ready to step in.

Two years after we met Kenny, he died of cardiac arrest. Heart problems are common among adults with Down syndrome. Knowing that did not ease the pain. We missed seeing Kenny when we entered church every Sunday. We missed his warm greetings. The children missed having him sit with them at the children's sermon. The entire congregation missed seeing him carry the cross and assisting with the service. The first year after his death, not a Sunday went by that someone didn't say, "Oh, how I miss Kenny."

Sometimes in reading the stories of saints and other devoted Christians, we wonder, "How could anyone be so utterly faithful?" Catherine of Sienna took her dissatisfaction with the abuses in the church so seriously that she wrote to the pope, persuading him to make changes. Dietrich Bonhoeffer died for his efforts to oppose the Nazis. Martin Luther King Jr. was killed for his work to bring equality to all people. The prolific accomplishments of leaders like these are so extraordinary that their lives sometimes function as an unrealistic measure for our own. We may look at their example and say, "I could never do that." We may read their stories and sigh, wondering how anyone could find the vision and courage to accomplish so much in a lifetime.

And yet our Christian life is not a competition to discover who can do the best job of following Jesus. It is a journey. Throughout our daily walk with Jesus, the challenge is to be faithful. Jesus commands his disciples, "If any want to become my followers, let them deny themselves and take up their cross daily and follow me" (Luke 9:23). Jesus does not require tremendous acts of devotion. He simply asks his followers to choose each day to follow him. And so, the Christian journey is most often made up of tiny steps rather than great strides. With our small acts of faithfulness, Jesus can weave a beautiful life that witnesses to God's love.

It's like the miracle story recorded in John's Gospel in which Jesus feeds more than five thousand people. The crowds were hungry and the disciples were doubtful. They didn't know where they would find enough bread to feed everyone. Andrew said, "There is a boy here who has five barley loaves and two fish. But what are they among so many people?" (John 6:9). Jesus took the boy's food, and with it he fed the whole crowd. Looking at the boy's offering, Andrew remarked how paltry it seemed in comparison to what they needed. And yet, small as the offering was, Jesus was able to make it enough. More than enough.

In our own lives, we might think that our offerings are inadequate. But that is not our worry. We are called to use our gifts to serve. We do this in many ways—some small and unseen, others very visible. Neither should we spend time fretting about what God might do with our gifts. Our task is to share our lunch, to give of ourselves faithfully day by day.

Kenny's life was a testimony to how choosing to be faithful in small ways leaves behind a great witness to Jesus. Kenny didn't discover a cure for cancer or write a theological treatise. He carried the cross into church on Sunday. He greeted people. He stood in front of the congregation, listening eagerly to the children's sermon. In many little ways, Kenny was faithful. And in doing so, he obeyed Jesus' command to take up his cross and follow.

On the Sunday after Kenny's death, we used the children's sermon time to talk about his life. We remembered the things we loved about him. We considered the many ways that he had pointed us to Jesus. Then we decided to thank God for the most precious gift of Kenny, another Christian who shared our path for too brief a time. The whole congregation sang in unison, so loud that even those sleeping across the street could hear, the words of the popular hymn "Lift High the Cross."

Questions for Reflection or Discussion

1. Reflect on some examples of God's working great things from someone's small, yet faithful actions.
2. In what ways do you faithfully serve God and others?
3. What are some of the small ways in which you could be serving God and others that you have been overlooking?

Challenge

Make a list of the people who, by their small and faithful acts, have significantly affected your life for the better.

Say a prayer of thanks for each person on your list.

Choose at least one person and write him or her a thank-you note.

32

It Takes a Lifetime

Mark 8:27–33

We are worshiping with the fifth-grade church school class. When we stand and speak the Apostles' Creed, ten-year-old Jeffrey holds the service book, leans toward us, and whispers, "Hey! I know this by heart!" He then covers the words with his hands, reciting the creed perfectly, proving to us that he really was paying attention in church school.

One of our seminary worship professors encouraged us to learn the prayers and hymns of the church. And he meant commit them to memory. Teach the congregations you serve to memorize scripture and the hymns of the church. They will be able to take these words into their family conflicts, into their hospital beds, into their most fearful moments.

Our professor was right. Knowing the words has made a difference. It has helped us when we worship. It has even helped in moments of frustration and anger when the closest words to our lips were not always the most profitable.

Still, there's more to learning the faith than memorizing the words of scripture, prayers, and hymns. Being able to recite the Apostles' Creed at age ten does not mean that we completely comprehend what it means—or all that it means for us. There's more to knowing God than knowing what the Christian church teaches about God. Knowing God takes a lifetime.

Some of us are introduced to God early in life. We begin to know God by name as our parents tell us the stories of scripture—the accounts of God's mighty deeds that have been passed down from generation to generation. We may attend church school, worship with family and friends, and learn how to spend quiet moments in prayer and study. All of these are ways in which we begin to know God. And getting to know God takes a lifetime.

It certainly took the disciples a while to know Jesus. Time and again he taught them, and yet time and again they failed to understand who he was. One day, as they traveled, Jesus asked, "Who do you say that I am?" (Mark 8:29). Like a diligent student, Peter answered correctly, "You are the Messiah." But then Peter proceeded to rebuke Jesus for talking about his impending death and resurrection. Peter knew the correct words to say, knew them by heart, but he didn't know what it meant for Jesus to be his Savior. He needed more time to comprehend Jesus' words, to make room for them in his heart and mind.

We need time too. A friend reported hearing her three-year-old daughter, Lindsay, mutter to herself before bed, over and over, "Jesus is God, Jesus is God." Lindsay was teaching herself, trying to understand and remember a difficult concept.

A twelve-year-old friend, knowing that we are pastors, repeatedly questioned us about the Christian doctrine of the Trinity. We explained. Again and again we painted the picture of this three-in-one God. At least we tried to. Sarah kept saying, "This doesn't make sense. What you are saying is impossible."

Lindsay and Sarah point out something else about knowing God—God is a mystery, beyond our complete understanding. Even if we knew everything that has been revealed to us about God, even if we could retain all that information, we would still be confronted with a mystery. Knowing God isn't like learning the multiplication table. There is so much more to know and so much we will never understand.

And yet the most important knowledge we can ever have about God is first learned by many of us when we are children: "Jesus loves us, this we know." It is a lesson we learn and relearn throughout all the stages of our lives. It is a fact that brings us comfort, whether we are four and afraid of the shadows beneath our bed or eighty-four and afraid to walk in the valley of the shadow of death. It is a concept that the youngest child can grasp in an instant, yet even the wisest among us will need an eternity to understand.

Questions for Reflection or Discussion
1. What are your earliest memories of getting to know God?
2. Who has helped you to know God better?
3. What about God is still a mystery to you?

Challenge
Look at the following Bible passages that describe basic Christian beliefs about God. Think about how you have experienced the message of each passage differently at various stages in life (e.g., as a child, teenager, and adult). You may want to record your reflections in a journal or discuss them with a friend.
1. Psalm 23
2. Romans 8:28
3. 1 Corinthians 10:13